W9-CRM-297

DISCARD

MENTAL ACTS

THEIR CONTENT AND THEIR OBJECTS

STUDIES IN
PHILOSOPHICAL PSYCHOLOGY

Edited by
R. F. HOLLAND

MENTAL ACTS

THEIR CONTENT
AND THEIR OBJECTS

BY

PETER GEACH

LONDON
ROUTLEDGE & KEGAN PAUL
NEW YORK: HUMANITIES PRESS

*First published in Great Britain 1957
by Routledge & Kegan Paul Ltd
Broadway House, 68-74 Carter Lane
London, E.C.4*

*Second impression 1960
Third impression 1964
Fourth impression 1967*

*Printed in Great Britain
by Billing & Sons, Limited
Guildford and London*

CONTENTS

CONTENTS ix

1

ACT, CONTENT, AND OBJECT

THE TITLE I have chosen for this work is a mere label for a set of problems; the controversial views that have historically been expresssed by using the terms "act", "content", and "object" ought not at the outset to be borne in mind. My own use of the term "mental act" may be explained, sufficiently for present purposes, as follows. In historical or fictional narrative there occur reports, not only of what human beings overtly said and did, but also of what they thought, how they felt, what they saw and heard, and so on; I shall call the latter kind of reports "reports of mental acts". The psychological character or, as I shall say, the *content* of mental acts is expressed by the use of various psychological verbs, such as "see", "hear", "hope", "think". Many of these psychological verbs require a grammatical object—a noun, noun-phrase, or noun-clause—to complete their sense. The hero sees *the postman coming*, hears *his knock*, hopes (has a sudden pang of hope) for *a letter from his sweetheart*, thinks *that his letter to her may have been opened by her guardian*, and so on. The use of such expressions is thus essential in stating the content of many mental acts; we may call them "object-expressions".

I shall avoid such uses of the term "object" as "A letter from his sweetheart is an object of the hero's

1

hope" or "The possibility of his letters' being inter-
cepted by her guardian is an object of his thought".
Familiar and understandable as such uses are, they raise
logical difficulties that I prefer to avoid. (One of these
difficulties is that the so-called object may not exist;
in my examples, there may be no letter from the hero's
sweetheart such as he hopes for, and no such possibility
as he thinks, of her guardian's intercepting his letters;
so the use of "object" that I shall avoid might easily
lead us on to such odd statements as "some objects of
mental acts do not exist".) I shall accordingly state my
problems not in the form "What sort of objects do
these mental acts have?" but rather in the form "Such-
and-such object-expressions are used in describing
these mental acts; what is the logical role of these
expressions?"

2

WITTGENSTEIN'S ALLEGED
REJECTION OF MENTAL ACTS

THE EXISTENCE of mental acts, as I have explained the term, ought not to be a matter of con-
troversy. According to the Gospel story, something
happened to St Peter when the cock crew; he heard it
crow, and he remembered Christ's prophecy of his
three denials; his hearing and his remembering were
mental acts. There is indeed a danger that when we
speak of mental acts or mental events or what happened in a person's mind, we may be led to an illegiti-
mate assimilation of psychological to physical reports.

There are logical similarities between the two kinds of reports, but there are no less important logical differences; these differences, on which Wittgenstein continually insisted, were already noticed by Aquinas, who remarked that when people speak of the mind as a 'subject of change' the meaning (*ratio*) of "subject" and "change" is quite other than it is in discourse about physical processes (Ia q. 75 art. 5 ad 2 um). But since such logical differences are just what we are looking out for in our enquiry, there is little risk of our forgetting that they may exist.

Wittgenstein has been understood as denying the existence of mental acts; and certain remarks of his about 'private objects' (WITTGENSTEIN, Part I, §293; Part II, p. 207) are very easily taken this way. I am sure, however, that I have not so far maintained anything Wittgenstein would have attacked. Of course Wittgenstein did not want to deny the obvious truth that people have a 'private' mental life, in the sense that they have for example thoughts they do not utter and pains they do not show; nor did he try to analyse away this truth in a neo-behaviouristic fashion. In one of his lectures he mentioned Lytton Strachey's imaginative description of Queen Victoria's dying thoughts. He expressly repudiated the view that such a description is meaningless because 'unverifiable'; it has meaning, he said, but only through its connexion with a wider, public, 'language-game' of describing people's thoughts; he used the simile that a chess-move worked out in a sketch of a few squares on a scrap of paper has significance through its connexion with the whole practice of playing chess. It is useful to observe Frege's distinction of sense (*Sinn*) and reference (*Bedeutung*) in stating Wittgenstein's position; what Wittgenstein wanted to deny was not the private *reference* of psychological expressions—e.g. that "pain" stands for a kind of experience that may be quite 'private'—but the possibility of giving them a private *sense*—e.g. of giving sense to the word "pain" by just attending to one's own pain-experiences, a performance that would be private and uncheckable. The view that psychological words are given a sense in this way is part of a theory (*abstractionism*, as I shall call it) which Wittgenstein rejected *in toto* and not only as regards psychological terms. Another view he rejected (one closely bound up, I believe, with an abstractionist view of psychological terms) is the view that such relations as that between a pain and its symptoms or a thought and the words expressing it have nothing to do with our concept of *pain* or *thought* and are just established inductively. We shall discuss both these topics later on.

3

RYLE'S REJECTION OF MENTAL ACTS

ALTHOUGH I SHALL try to show that reports of mental acts are logically different from reports of physical events, I hold that reports of both kinds are categorical. This view is sharply opposed to Ryle's view that psychological statements are not reports of private events (mental acts) but are hypothetical or semi-hypothetical statements about overt behaviour. (RYLE, pp. 33, 46.) I shall not criticize Ryle's attempted analyses in detail; the entire programme seems to me misconceived. In the first place, he makes no serious attempt to carry out his programme consistently; he leaves some reports of mental acts standing, without offering any analysis of them into hypothetical or semi-hypothetical statements about behaviour. The mental acts in question are indeed referred to throughout in a highly depreciatory style, as "itches", "tingles", "tweaks", "agitations", etc.; but this rhetorical trick proves nothing. If reports of these mental acts cannot be reduced to hypothetical or semi-hypothetical statements about overt behaviour, then the view that the distinction between categoricals and hypotheticals is *the* logical distinction between physical and psychological statements must be *completely* wrong. A logical principle allows of no exceptions—not even if the exceptions are events that only James Joyce would put into a novel.

Secondly, when Ryle explains a statement of an *actual* difference between two men's mental states as really asserting only that there are circumstances in which one *would* act differently from the other, and apparently holds that this could be *all* the difference there is between the two, he is running counter to a very deep-rooted way of thinking. When two agents differ in their behaviour, we look for some actual, not merely hypothetical, difference between them to account for this; as the scholastics said, *omne agens agit in quantum est in actu.* Ryle explicitly and repeatedly compares psychological accounts of behaviour to saying that a glass broke because it was brittle (had the dispositional property of brittleness); in so doing, however, he is setting them on a level with the statement that opium puts people to sleep because it has a dormitive power—which I believe was not his intention. (RYLE, pp. 50, 86–7, 88–9, *et al.*)

The principle expressed in the scholastic tag just cited is of importance in scientific investigation. A physicist would be merely impatient if somebody said to him: "Why look for, or postulate, any *actual* difference between a magnetized and an unmagnetized bit of iron? Why not just say that if certain things are done to a bit of iron certain hypotheticals become true of it?" He would be still more impatient at being told that his enquiries were vitiated by the logical mistake of treating "*x* is magnetized" as categorical, whereas it is really hypothetical or semi-hypothetical. Of course there may be people prepared to say that, although men of science regularly look for differences already existing between the agents in order to explain differences of behaviour, there is no reason to expect that such differences always do exist; the principle on which men of science proceed might be as unsound as any gambling system, and their success up to now mere luck. I shall not argue the point.

We may well be reluctant, then, to expound in Ryle's fashion even psychological accounts of *actual* differences in behaviour. Our reluctance should be still greater when we are invited to regard a statement that two men, whose overt behaviour was not actually different, were in different states of mind (e.g. that one checked a column of figures with his mind on the job, the other with his mind on his domestic troubles) as being really a statement that the behaviour of one man *would have been* different from that of the other in hypothetical circumstances that never arose. It ought to be, but plainly is not, generally known to philosophers that the logic of counterfactual conditionals is a very ill-explored territory; no adequate formal logic for them has yet been devised, and there is an extensive literature on the thorny problems that crop up. It is really a scandal that people should count it a philosophical advance to adopt a programme of analysing ostensible categoricals into unfulfilled conditionals, like the programmes of phenomenalists with regard to 'physical-object' statements and of neo-behaviourists with regard to psychological statements.

With specious lucidity, Ryle describes the counterfactual conditionals he uses as having the 'sentence-job' not of stating facts but of licensing inferences. The terms "inference-licence" and "inference-ticket" seem to be explanatory because we associate them with very familiar institutions. In order to see that nothing has been explained at all, we need only ask the question what inferences from fact to fact a counterfactual conditional does give us licence to perform. I need hardly comment on Ryle's view that "the rubber has begun to lose its elasticity" has to do not with a change in the rubber but with the (incipient?) expiry of an inference-ticket. (See RYLE, pp. 120–5.)

4

ACTS OF JUDGMENT

THE SORT of mental acts that I shall chiefly investigate are acts of judgment. This is not an arbitrary choice. Concepts, as we shall see, are capacities exercised in acts of judgment—psychological concepts, in psychological judgments about oneself and others; and one of the chief obstacles we shall encounter is a tangle of mistakes and confusions about

B

judgments and concepts generally, by reason of which
people go widely astray in their account of psychological judgments and concepts in particular. I hope
my work on the nature of judgment will do something
to clear away the tangle.

Many readers may wish to object *in limine* that even
if there are mental acts, there certainly are not acts of
judgment. However difficult the logic of dispositional
words may be, it is surely clear both that "believe" is
such a word, and that the acts which make it true to
say that So-and-so believes such-and-such are not only,
perhaps not at all, acts of judgment. A gardener's belief that it will rain is a disposition exercised in suitable
acts of preparation rather than in intermittent mental
acts of judgment. (RYLE, pp. 175–6.)

But is there in fact any behaviour characteristic of
a given belief? Can action be described as "acting as if
you held such-and-such a belief" unless we take for
granted, or are somehow specially informed about, the
needs and wants of the agent? In Ryle's example this
information is smuggled in by his speaking of a *gardener's* rain-expecting behaviour (and tacitly assuming
that the gardener is not e.g. a discontented or corrupt
servant who wants the garden to be ruined). When
Dr Johnson did penance in Uttoxeter market-place, he
may have begun by standing around bareheaded until
the threatened shower should fall; this would not be
recognizable as rain-expecting behaviour without a
knowledge of Johnson's wish to do penance. There is
indeed one sort of behaviour that does characterize a
belief—namely, putting it into words; lying is necessarily the exception, not the rule. But putting your
belief into words is one of those 'intellectualistic' activi-
ties that Ryle seeks to depreciate. In this instance, his

doing so is very understandable; for on the face of it if somebody puts his belief into words, not parrotwise but with consideration, then there occurs a mental act, of the sort that I call an act of judgment. Anybody performs an act of judgment at least as often as he makes up his mind how to answer a question; and acts of judgment in this sense are plainly episodic—have a position in a time-series. (We shall see, indeed, that we cannot—cannot in principle, not for lack of information or technique—assign positions in time to acts of judgment in the same way as we do to physical events, nor even in the same way as we do to sensations. But this is irrelevant to our present discussion.)

In very many languages, a report of an act of judgment is expressed by using the *oratio obliqua* construction—i.e. the same construction as is used with 'verbs of saying' to report the gist or upshot of somebody's remark rather than the actual words he used. Thus, in English and Latin and many other languages (including, as a pupil once told me, some African languages), there need be no difference except in the main verb between a statement that James *said* it was time for everybody to go home and a statement that James *judged* it was time for everybody to go home. And for every judgment whose content can thus be given by means of a piece of *oratio obliqua*, there is some form of words, in the language considered, that would be suitable to *express* the act of judgment—namely, some form of words whose gist is given in the piece of *oratio obliqua*. (We must of course distinguish between expressing a judgment and expressing a *report* of a judgment. "James judged that the crevasse was too wide for him to jump" expresses a *report* of James's judgment; a form of words suitable to express this act of judgment would be "the crevasse is too wide for me to jump".)

Now given a statement made by James in a language L, the grammatical rules of L generally allow us to construct a piece of *oratio obliqua* that preserves the gist of the statement. (Schoolboys often do this as an exercise in Latin grammar.) Having done this, we need only tack on the expression in L for "James judged (that . . .)", and we have a report in L of the judgment expressed in James's original statement. Moreover, if we have sufficient mastery of L to understand both the expression for "James judged (that . . .)" and the piece of *oratio obliqua*, we shall understand the report so constructed, no matter what the actual sense of the remark done into *oratio obliqua* may be.

Nonsense cannot be turned into *oratio obliqua*; for *oratio obliqua*, which serves to report the upshot of what is said, cannot be used to report nonsense. So an attempt to report that somebody judges nonsense is itself nonsense. A British pupil of Heidegger might say "Nothing noths" in a tone of conviction; assuming that this is nonsense, "he judged that Nothing nothed" would also be nonsense. (We ought rather to say: "he judged that "Nothing noths" was the expression of a truth".)

These remarks about the expression of judgments and the reports of judgments may appear very obvious; but in fact, as we shall see, they impose severe logical restrictions upon analyses of judgment.

5

THE NATURE OF CONCEPTS

CONCEPTS, the old-fashioned logic-books tell us, are presupposed to, and exercised in, acts of judgment. Of course this is psychology, not logic; but I think that it is correct psychology.

It has been argued, however, that, so far from concepts' being presupposed to judgments, the common feature of judgments in which one and the same concept is supposed to be exercised is something that appears on its own account only in subsequent reflection on the judgments. I do not, it is said, first acquire a concept of *man* and then put it to work in forming judgments about *man* (judgments whose natural expression in English would contain a use of the word "man"); on the contrary, I first of all form certain judgments and then, reflecting upon them, bring them under the head "judgments about *man*"; this feature that I now attend to on its own account did not exist as an independent factor in the original judgments.

My reply is as follows. Any reportable act of judgment is apt for verbal expression, in a form of words whose gist is contained in the *oratio obliqua* of the report. (I am not asserting, nor do I think, that an act of judgment is always put into words, even 'in the head'). Let us concentrate, for the moment, on judgments that are verbally expressed. The sentence expressing a judgment will consist of a number of words; and the significant utterance of the sentence therefore brings into exercise various relatively simple skills—

the abilities to use the various expressions that occur in the sentence. It is important to notice that as applied to whole sentences the philosophical slogan "the meaning of an expression is its use" is seriously mistaken; at any rate if "use" is here taken to mean "established usage". For in general there is no established usage for a sentence as a whole; e.g. the sentences in this book do not get their meaning from any established usage, nor have I learned to use them in circles where they were commonly used. It is words and phrases that have an established usage; a language is mastered not by learning whole sentences out of a guidebook but by learning to make up sentences in it and to understand sentences not previously heard. That is how we learn foreign languages, and how children come to understand and speak their native language.[1] The ability to express a judgment in words thus presupposes a number of capacities, previously acquired, for intelligently using the several words and phrases that make up the sentence. I shall apply the old term "concepts" to these special capacities—an application which I think lies fairly close to the historic use of the term. It will be a *sufficient* condition for James's having the concept of *so-and-so* that he should have mastered the intelligent use (including the use in made-up sentences) of a word for *so-and-so* in some language. Thus: if somebody knows how to use the English word "red", he has a concept of red; if he knows how to use the first-person pronoun, he has a concept of *self*; if he knows how to use the nega-

[1] Psychologists appear not to take this fact sufficiently into account. Thus, Humphrey takes as his example of the use of language, not a sentence devised for a new situation, but an ejaculation "Rain!" when it is raining; not surprisingly he concludes that the problem of meaning is just a case of the problem of learned responses. (HUMPHREY, pp. 227–34.)

tive construction in some language, he has a concept of negation.

An analogy from playing chess may help to show how concepts and acts of judgment are related. Making an appropriate move from a certain position may be, and at the opening of the game very likely will be, a learned response; but in the middle game it will certainly not be so, for the position may well occur only once in a life-time of play. On the other hand, the ability to make an appropriate move from a given position always presupposes a number of simpler, previously acquired, skills— the capacities to carry out the moves and captures that are lawful for the pawns and the various pieces. As these skills are related to the chess-move, so concepts are related to the act of judgment.

I have stated only a sufficient, not a necessary, condition for somebody's having a given concept. If a man struck with aphasia can still play bridge or chess, I certainly wish to say he still has the concepts involved in the game, although he can no longer exercise them verbally. But it would be hard to devise non-verbal criteria for the patient's having retained a concept of *the day after tomorrow*. The central and typical applications of the term "having a concept" are those in which a man is master of a bit of linguistic usage; we can then reasonably extend the term to cases sufficiently like these, e.g. where the man can play 'intellectual' games like bridge and chess. I shall not try to draw any sharp line between what is 'sufficiently like' the central and typical cases and what is not; I do not think we shall go far wrong if we concentrate henceforward on concepts exercised linguistically.

A concept, as I am using the term, is subjective—it is a mental capacity belonging to a particular person.

(My use of "concept" is thus to be contrasted e.g. with Russell's use of it in *The Principles of Mathematics* and again with the use of it to translate Frege's "*Begriff*"; Russell's 'concepts' and Frege's *Begriffe* were supposed to be objective entities, not belonging to a particular mind.) The subjective nature of concepts does not however imply that it is improper to speak of two people as " having the same concept "; conformably to my explanation of the term "concept", this will mean that they have the same mental capacity, i.e. can do essentially the same things. Thus, if each of two men has mastered the intelligent use of the negative construction in his own language, we may say that they have the same mental capacity, the same concept; they both have the concept of negation. There are of course all degrees of transition between cases where we should say unhesitatingly "they have different words, but they use them in the same way; they have the same concept", and where we should rather say "it's not just a verbal difference; they have different concepts".

I thus accept the psychology of the old logic-books, to the extent of recognizing the possession of concepts as presupposed to acts of judgment, and regarding a judgment as the exercise of a number of concepts. A feature of the traditional theory that I find unacceptable is the doctrine that there are acts of 'simple apprehension', in which concepts are somehow exercised *singly* without being applied to anything. I think these acts are mythical; in chess one can practise the moves of a solitary man on the board, but I think there is no analogous exercise of a single unapplied concept.

Having criticized Ryle for his reckless use of the term " disposition ", I may myself be criticized for introducing concepts, which are supposed to be capacities. But to say that a man has a certain concept is to say that he *can* perform, because he sometimes *does* perform, mental exercises of a specifiable sort. This way of using the modal word "can" is a minimal use, confined to a region where the logic of the word is as clear as possible. *Ab esse ad posse valet consequentia*— what is can be, what a man does he can do; that is clear if anything in modal logic is clear, and no more than this is involved in my talking of concepts. Ryle's attempt to expound ostensible statements about actual mental states in terms of complicated sets of subjunctive conditionals is a far more dubious undertaking.

The exercise of a given concept in an act of judgment is not in general a definite, uniform sort of mental act; it does not even make sense to ask just how many concepts are exercised in a given judgment. Our chess analogy may here again be of service, in showing why this question is unreasonable. Playing chess involves a number of abilities, which are not only distinguishable but can actually exist separately; for one way of teaching chess would be to play first just with the kings and the pawns and then add the other pieces successively in later games. It would, however, be absurd to ask just how many of these abilities there were, or just how many were exercised in a particular move; although one might perfectly well say that somebody knew the knight's move, and that this knowledge was or was not exercised in a particular move. Our language about the concepts exercised in a given act of judgment makes sense or does not make sense in much the same way.

In discussing (as for the most part I shall) concepts that are involved in the intelligent use of words, I shall often have to use the phrases "to know the use of the

word ——", "to know the way to use the word ——",
and the like. These phrases are irritatingly ambiguous,
but practically indispensable. One ambiguity of them
is notorious: ambiguity as between being able to use a
word intelligently and being able to give an account of
its use—between *knowing how* and *knowing that*; I shall
consistently keep to the *knowing how* sense unless the
contrary is expressly stated. Another, trickier, ambiguity may be brought out by this question: if a Frenchman who knows no English knows the use of the French
adjective "rouge", does he know the use of the English
adjective "red"? In one sense of "knowing the use of
the word" he must know the use of the word "red",
because it is *the same as* the (relevant) use of the word
"rouge", which *ex hypothesi* he knows. In another sense,
he does not 'know the use of' any English word, because he knows no English. The former sense of the
phrase "know the use of the word "red" " might be
brought out by saying: "know how to use *some* word
in the way that the word "red" is in fact used in English"; but to avoid clumsily long clauses I shall express
this sense just by saying: "know the use of the word
"red" ", and shall avoid using such expressions in
the sense in which they are truly predicable only of
English-speaking persons. (I am afraid some recent
philosophers have often been ensnared by this latter
ambiguity of "knowing the use of a word"; and so they
give us tedious and inaccurate supplements to *Modern
English Usage*, instead of philosophical discussion of a
'way of using a word' which could be found in many
languages.)

Many psychologists, wishing to use the term "concept" far more widely than I do, would strongly object
to my concentrating on concepts expressed in language;

they would say that an animal has acquired a concept if it has learned a discriminative response to some feature of its environment. If a rat or a dog is trained to react in a certain way whenever it has a triangle shown to it (rather than some other shape), then they would say it has acquired a concept of *triangle*. (Earthworms, we are told, regularly pull bits of paper into their burrows by the sharpest angles; I do not know whether any psychologist would be prepared on this account to say earthworms have an innate concept of angular magnitude.) What is at issue here is not just the way the term "concept" is to be used, but the desirability of comparing these achievements of rats and dogs with the performances of human beings who possess a concept of *triangle*; the psychologists I am criticizing want to play down the differences between human and animal performances, and I want to stress them. The life of brutes lacks so much that is integral to human life that it can only be misleading to say that they have concepts like us—as misleading as it would be to say that men have tails and women lay eggs (as I have actually heard someone of strong 'evolutionist' opinions say in discussion) or to call the noises made by brutes "language". Experience in training dogs to 'recognize' triangles can be no guide in (let us say) teaching geometry. It is scholasticism in the worst sense of the word to argue that if men are descended from brutes they *cannot* have anything that the brutes did not already possess (*nihil dat quod non habet!*); the argument is just as bad whether it is used to disprove evolution (as it actually once used to be—JAMES, vol. II, pp. 670–1), or to prove that brutes, from whom man is descended, *must* have concepts at least in a 'rudimentary' form.

6

ABSTRACTIONISM

I SHALL USE "abstractionism" as a name for the doctrine that a concept is acquired by a process of singling out in attention some one feature given in direct experience—*abstracting* it—and ignoring the other features simultaneously given—*abstracting from* them. The abstractionist would wish to maintain that all acts of judgment are to be accounted for as exercises of concepts got by abstraction; but he is often driven into allowing exceptions for certain kinds of concepts, because in their case abstractionism is palpably unreasonable. My own view is that abstractionism is wholly mistaken; that no concept at all is acquired by the supposed process of abstraction.

My refutation of abstractionism will make no appeal to the empirical data collected by professional child psychologists. My procedure may thus appear to many readers arrogantly *a priori*. Surely the origins of anything have to be discovered empirically; what is the use of arguing without information? But since acquiring a concept is a process of becoming able *to do something*, an enquiry as to the origin of a concept may be vitiated from the start by wrong analysis of *what is done* when the concept is exercised; and such an error may be shown without any empirical data as to concept-formation in children. Again, as Wittgenstein remarked, the connexion between *learning* and *being able* to do something is not just an empirical one; for we should plainly not be willing to call *any* process that ended in ability to do something "learning" to do it.

Of course we cannot work out in our heads how abilities are acquired; but there are conceivable ways of acquiring them to which we should unhesitatingly refuse to apply the term "learning". If, as in a story of Stephen Leacock's, a boy could come to know Latin by submitting to a brain operation, he would not have *learned* Latin from the surgeon. Now abstractionism is a theory of how certain mental performances are *learned*; the discussion I am entering upon is designed to show that the processes alleged by abstractionists would not be a *learning* of how to make these mental acts. Moreover, I shall try to show that the whole idea of abstraction—of discriminative attention to some feature given in experience—is thoroughly incoherent; if I succeed, no notice need any longer be taken of claims that abstractionism has experimental support. No experiment can either justify or straighten out a confusion of thought; if we are in a muddle when we design an experiment, it is only to be expected that we should ask Nature cross questions and she return crooked answers.

Abstractionism has played an important role in the history of philosophy; but it is not this that concerns us—the doctrine is very much alive. (See PRICE *passim* and HUMPHREY, chap. ix.) Two applications of abstractionism are of special interest: to concepts of sensible things, and to psychological concepts. The first application came into vogue during the decadence of scholasticism: concepts of sensible things have to be formed by picking out features directly given in sense-experience (*nihil in intellectu nisi prius in sensu*), so that we cannot form any 'proper' concepts of kinds of substance, like gold and water, nor of *substance* as such; the word "substance" will stand for 'something we know not what', and kinds of substance will be conceived only by piecing together 'proper' concepts of their characteristic sensible features. (It is mere ignorance to make Locke the originator of this style of talk; in his day it was the commonest scholastic claptrap, and this bad tradition still survives in certain quarters.) Such a view as to our knowledge of substance is grossly incoherent; what ought to be inferred on these premises is not that "substance" means something, we know not what, but that it means nothing; for assuredly we can find no discriminable feature of our sense-experience answering to the word "substance", so there ought not, on the view we are considering, to be any concept answering to it either. And similarly an abstractionist ought to hold that when we think of gold or water our thoughts must somehow be fadged up out of sense-given elements; the concepts exercised must be concepts of features given in sense-experience like wetness and yellowness, and will not include a special concept of *substance*. In fact this consistently abstractionist view of substance-concepts is now pretty generally held.

As regards psychological concepts, there is a scholastic tradition in which the maxim "*nihil in intellectu nisi prius in sensu*" was strictly applied to them; they were supposed to be analogical developments of concepts acquired in the first instance by performing abstraction upon sense-experience. I shall return to this doctrine of analogical development of concepts at a later stage; it is not necessarily connected with abstractionism, and is indeed open to serious objection on abstractionist premises. Let us suppose that we use a word C originally to express our concept of a recognizable characteristic *c* found in sense-experience, and then go on to use C in a transferred, psychological, sense. The new use of the word C will express recognition, not of the sensible characteristic c, but of some psychological characteristic γ; only because we do recognize γ as a feature of our mental life can we see the suitability of expressing this recognition by the metaphorical use of the term C. But if we do thus recognize γ, then we can in principle have a 'proper' concept of γ, independent of any 'analogy' between γ and c.—This objection seems to me pretty conclusive from an abstractionist point of view; if any sense is to be made of the idea that psychological concepts are developed by 'analogy', it must be freed from its connexion with abstractionism.

The characteristic abstractionist view of psychological concepts is that they are abstractively derived from *inner* experience; we are supposed to possess a quasi-sense that is related to psychical occurrences in much the same way as our senses are to physical occurrences; and just as we form a concept of *red* by discriminatively attending to, and performing abstraction upon, visual experience, so we form a concept of *judging* or *desiring* by discriminatively attending to, and performing abstraction upon, the deliverances of this 'introspective' quasi-sense. The classical statement of this doctrine is to be found in Locke (*Essay*, II. i. 4); it is a doctrine still widely held—at least, many people still talk and argue as if it were true. (The quasi-sense is compared sometimes to seeing—intro-*spection*— sometimes to feeling; sometimes we are supposed to learn what judging and desiring are by taking a quick inward look and catching ourselves in the act of judging or desiring, and sometimes, by the way we feel when performing these acts.)

I shall discuss later on the peculiar difficulties of 'inner sense'; if this doctrine cannot be maintained, then abstractionism must be abandoned also, at least as regards psychological concepts. (We have seen already that a serious attempt to make out that such concepts are developed 'analogically' from concepts applicable in sense-experience would oblige us to go outside the limits of abstractionism.) Conversely, if we see reason to reject abstractionism altogether, even for concepts like that of *red*, then we shall have overcome the strongest inducement to describe self-knowledge in terms of inner 'sense'; for there will no longer be any tendency to think that psychological concepts must be got 'abstractively' from something like sense-experience.

7

ABSTRACTIONISM AND LOGICAL CONCEPTS

ABSTRACTIONISTS rarely attempt an abstractionist account of logical concepts, like those of *some*, *or*, and *not*; they will usually admit that such concepts are a special case to which abstractionism does not apply. There have, however, been some attempts to explain even logical concepts as obtained by abstraction (as in RUSSELL (4) and PRICE). These attempts appeal to 'inner sense' as the material from which logical concepts are to be extracted. Such an appeal could hardly be avoided; for logical concepts are not to be explained as the result of performing abstraction upon any sense-experience. In the sensible world you will find no specimens of alternativeness and negativeness from which you could form by abstraction the concept of *or* or of *not*. The sort of concept applicable in the sensible world that is plausibly representable as got by abstraction is the sort that could in favourable circumstances be conveyed by ostensive definition; the word answering to the concept could be used to label a specimen of what the concept applies to, or a picture of such a specimen. But nowhere in the sensible world could you find anything, nor could you draw any picture, that could suitably be labelled "or" or "not". Hence the abstractionist appeals to 'inner sense' as the source of logical concepts: "or" gets its meaning through our performing abstraction upon experiences of hesitation, and "not" is similarly related to experiences of frustration or inhibition (stopping oneself from doing things), and so on. So far as I can tell, these abstractionist views as to logical concepts being got out of inner experiences are based upon the feelings that happen to be aroused in a particular writer when he says a logical word over and over to himself—a magical rite of evoking its meaning. (For a conspicuous example of this, see JAMES, vol. I, pp. 245–6, 252–3.) To many people, such recitation of the word "or" suggests a feeling of dithering between alternatives; to me, on the other hand, it naturally suggests a threat— "——, *or else* ——!" Would an abstractionist be willing to say on that account that my concept of *or* was different from the others'? He surely ought to say so, on his own premises. But in fact the coherency of other men's language, and the possibility of communicating with them, should be conclusive proof that all have the same logical concepts (in the sense of "same concepts" explained in the last Section but one); idiosyncratic

c

feelings produced by logical words are neither here
nor there. Of course in the living use of such words,
as opposed to the recitation of them, such feelings
may be wholly absent, without the words' being
in any way deprived of meaning by their absence. I
very much doubt whether anybody either dithers or
feels threatened when he contemplates the statement
that every number is odd *or* even.

Russell's attempted account of "every S is P" is
highly instructive. A judgment that a definite individual, A, is a swan and is not white would consist in
my applying my concept *swan* to A but stopping myself from applying my concept *white* to A. I can now
abstract what would be common to the possible judgments that A is a swan and not white, that B is a swan
and not white, and so on; this gives me the content of a
possible judgment that *something* is a swan and not
white. If I now inhibit myself from making this judgment (whose content is derived, by abstraction, from
the contents of certain possible judgments that would
themselves involve my inhibiting myself from doing
something) then I am judging that *nothing* is a swan
without being white, i.e. that *every* swan is white.
Russell thinks it is quite fair play to use inhibition of
an inhibition as part of his apparatus; has not Pavlov
studied pre-verbal forms of this operation in dogs?
(RUSSELL (4), p. 255; *cf.* also pp. 88–90 on "some".)

A professional psychologist may well protest that
Russell's account just exhibits the characteristic weak-
nesses of a logician trying to do psychology, and is too
obviously wrong to be of any interest. But the logical
part of Russell's analysis is right: "every S is P" does
mean the same as "no S is not P", and this is the negation of "some S is not P". The trouble arises rather

from Russell's abstractionist accounts of negation and "some"; since his account as a whole is clearly wrong, and the logical part of it is right, we ought to reject abstractionism about logical concepts.

The attempt to relate logical words to inner experiences and feelings thus breaks down. For a convinced abstractionist, though, a possible alternative would be to deny that there are special logical concepts corresponding to the logical words. This is especially plausible as regards negation. Is it not a mere blind copying of language-structures to suppose that use of the term "not red" brings into play two distinct concepts—the concept *not* and the concept *red*? Surely what I exercise in using the term "not red" is simply the concept *red*; knowing what *is* red and knowing what *is not* red are inseparable—*eadem est scientia oppositorum*. The abstractionist might thus say that the problem how we get a concept of *not* is spurious; only concepts expressed in positive terms need to be explained, and for these abstractionism has not been shown to be inadequate. If concepts were fundamentally capacities for recognition, as abstractionists think they are, this argument would be decisive; for clearly we recognize the presence and the absence of a characteristic by one and the same capacity. (See PRICE, p. 123.[1]) But even apart from this special view as to the nature of concepts, it seems undeniable that in some sense the concept *red* is the very same mental capacity as the concept *not red*; and thus there seems to be no place for a special concept of negation—putting "not" before "red" would simply

---

[1] Oddly enough, on the very next page of his work Price slides into the view that negation is understood through abstraction performed on 'inner' experiences of frustration: "Disappointed expectation", he says, "is what brings NOT into our lives".

serve to distinguish a special exercise of the concept *red*.

If, however, we relate the concept *not* to judgments expressed in language, then I think we can see a justification for saying that there is such a distinct concept, since ability to use the word "not" intelligently is certainly a distinct mental ability. Again, students of elementary logic show ability to understand the word "not" in logical schemata, such as: "if every P is M, and some S is not M, then some S is not P". If "not" in "not red" were merely a signal for a special exercise of the concept *red*, our grasp of its meaning in such schemata would be inexplicable. We cannot say that "not" in "not M" is merely a signal for a special use of the concept expressed by "M"; for the schematic letter "M" does not express a concept, as "red" does.

Even if we consider non-linguistic performances in which concepts are exercised, we can still, I think, distinguish between exercise of the concept *red and not red* and exercise of the concept *not* as such. To sort a lot of pebbles into red ones and ones that are not red could be simply an exercise of the concept *red and not red*; and here it would be plainly silly to distinguish a concept of *red* and one of *not red* as distinct abilities. But now suppose that the sorter goes over his two heaps when the sorting is done, to see if there are any misplaced pebbles: the act of transferring a pebble to *the other* heap is an exercise of the concept of negation.

In describing the way that the concept *not* would show itself in the sorter's behaviour, I found it natural to use the word "other" (= Latin "*alter*", not "*alius*": "the other of two"). This concept of *other* is near akin to the concept of negation; and is equally inexplicable on abstractionist lines. There does not even seem to be a characteristic feeling of otherness; and there is certainly no feature common to all the things that are other. Yet this concept is easily and early arrived at; a child understands the use of "other hand" and "other foot" before it understands "right" and left", for which an abstractionist account is plausible.

The logical concepts must then, I think, be recognized as distinct mental abilities; and if so they do not admit of any abstractionist explanation. Such recognition of them does not commit us to trying to answer the question how many distinct logical concepts there are, or how many are exercised in a given act of judgment; we saw in the last Section but one that such questions are unreasonable.

8

ABSTRACTIONISM AND ARITHMETICAL CONCEPTS

THERE ARE very many concepts, of a more homely appearance than the logical concepts, for which abstractionism is no less unworkable. Number-concepts are one example. We are indeed often taught arithmetic in childhood by such procedures as putting three apples with two apples; and then later on we hear of the addition of 'abstract units'—"3 + 2 = 5" means, we are told, that three abstract units and two more make five in all. This is surely because abstractionism has invaded pedagogic theory and practice; the talk about 'abstract units' presumably means that "3 + 2 = 5" is taken as expressing the result of abstraction from the nature of the concrete units added, e.g. from their being apples. But this is one of the contexts in which the abstractionist talk of 'discriminative attention' is most obviously a muddled and indefensible way of talking. It may well be all right to say: "Don't bother about the shapes of the things I show you, just attend to their colours"; this is the sort of case that makes abstractionism plausible. But it is certainly a self-contradictory instruction to say: "Don't bother about what kind of things they are, just attend to their number". For a number is essentially a number *of* a kind of things; things are numerable only as belonging to a kind of things.[1] What number I find may vary, without my observations' varying, because I am considering a different kind of things; the same auditory experience may give me the number 2 if what I have in mind is *heroic couplets*, 4 if it is *lines of verse*, 40 if it is *syllables*, 25 if it is *words*; if I have no special kind of thing in mind, no number will suggest itself to me at all. (Of course, if I am shown a lot of apples and just told to count, the kind of things I shall think of will most likely be *apples*; but it need not be.) Thus number-concepts just cannot be got by concentrating on the number and abstracting from the kind of things that are being counted. Before applying a number-concept we must first apply the concept of some kind of things to the things that we count. This shows why number-concepts cannot be among the first to be acquired, and why there are languages of

[1] This truism is certainly what Frege intended to bring out in saying that a number attaches to a *Begriff*. What makes the truism worth enunciating is that people who would verbally assent to it are often sufficiently muddle-headed to say other things that are incompatible with it.

primitive peoples that are rich in words for kinds of things (corresponding to common nouns and adjectives in English) but very poor in numeral words.

Moreover, the elementary arithmetical operations cannot be coherently explained as being performed on collections of abstract units, or as what operations on concrete collections look like when we abstract from the special natures of such collections. Such an account superficially appears adequate for addition and subtraction; for multiplication and division it will not do at all. It sounds plausible to say that "$3 + 2 = 5$" and "$5 - 2 = 3$" describe features of putting-together and taking-away operations performable on pennies and conkers; features that we apprehend on their own account by abstracting from the pennies and the conkers. It is perhaps a bit less plausible to say that, by taking an operation performed on concrete units and abstracting from the concrete units, we can conceive an operation upon that many abstract units; still, whatever "abstract unit" means, surely "three conkers and two more are five conkers" remains true when for "conkers" we substitute "abstract units". But it does not in the same way look like sense to talk of getting six abstract units by multiplying two abstract units into three abstract units, or of getting two abstract units by dividing three abstract units into six abstract units; nor are there any operations with pennies that would enable us to give such talk a sense when once we had abstracted from the pennies. To talk of raising two abstract units to the power of three abstract units is, if possible, even worse nonsense; and no manipulations of three pennies will teach a child what the exponent "3" means. In teaching arithmetic, the idea that the number n consists of n abstract units is not just logically open to exception, or lacking in rigour; it is quite unusable in practice.

Even at the level of school arithmetic, a child needs to master a way of talking about the number n which has nothing to do with groups of n concrete or abstract units—viz. in expressions of the form "doing a thing n times over". Exponentiation has to be explained this way; 2 to the power of 3 is 1 multiplied 3 times over by 2 ($1 \times 2 \times 2 \times 2$). The same thing is clear for multiplication and division. "$2 \times 3 = 6$" means that to add 2 to anything 3 times over is to add 6; "13 divided by 5 gives 2, remainder 3" means that from 13 you can subtract 5 *twice* over, the result being 3. Now this account could be used, instead of the nonsense about concrete and abstract units, for addition and subtraction too. Adding 5 to 7 can be explained as performing 5 times over upon the number 7 the operation of *going on to the next number*—(7), 8, 9, 10, 11, *12*. Subtraction is similarly explicable in terms of counting backwards. "This may be more correct logically than talking about abstract units", someone will protest, "but it is too difficult for children—it is psychologically unsound". But if a child finds "doing a thing so many times over" too difficult to understand, it will never acquire genuine number-concepts and never be able to do arithmetic at all. And learning to say number words when presented with groups of apples varying in number is not even to start learning what "to do a thing so many times over" means. To teach a child this, one would count, or get the child to count, while some action was repeatedly done.

Now the way counting is learned is wholly contrary to abstractionist preconceptions. What an abstractionist might call "abstract counting"—i.e. recitation of the successive numerals without counting any objects—is logically and temporally prior to counting objects; the series of numerals has to be learned before it can be applied. The first numerals ("one" to "twenty" in English) must indeed be learned parrot-wise to begin with, like "eany-meany-miny-mo"; but success in counting beyond this point depends on the child's practical grasp of a rule by which it could go on forming numerals indefinitely. (Such practical grasp of a rule of course does not imply ability to formulate it.) Young children sometimes amuse themselves by counting up to large numbers (several thousands); they have never heard their elders do this, and quite likely they will never in their lives have occasion to count so high for any practical purpose; the exercise of going on in the series of numerals is one that they find pleasur-able on its own account. The ability to do this is not yet possession of full-blown number-concepts, because the series of numerals has not yet any application; but the performance is a characteristic *intellectual* perform-ance. Moreover, the pattern of the numeral series that is thus grasped by the child exists nowhere in nature outside human languages; so the human race cannot possibly have discerned this pattern by abstracting it from some natural context. The practices of counting objects, and again of counting the repeated perform-ances of some action or operation, are developed on the basis of this 'abstract counting'; what has to be mastered here is the establishment of one-one corre-spondence between the numerals and the things or performances being counted—e.g. one gets the child to go on to the next numeral when and only when it goes up another stair of the staircase. The abstractionist doctrine that 'abstract numbers' are understood by

abstracting from the special nature of the things num-
bered puts the cart before the horse.

9

ABSTRACTIONISM AND
RELATIONAL CONCEPTS

OTHER CONCEPTS, less near akin to logical
concepts than number-concepts are, turn out to
resist abstractionist explanations. Consider the concepts *big* and *small*. Is there a common identifiable
feature shared by a big elephant, a big rat, and a big
flea, and which they do not share with a small elephant, a small rat, and a small flea? Can I pick this
feature out by discriminative attention, abstracting
from what kind of thing it is that I am calling big or
small? Certainly not; I cannot rightly apply the term
"big" or "small" unless I am meaning a big or small
thing of a certain kind. A big flea or rat is a small
animal, and a small elephant is a big animal. There can
be no question of ignoring the kind of thing to which
"big" or "small" is referred and forming a concept of
big or *small* by abstraction. It has indeed been pointed
out that I can recognize a thing as big or small of its
kind without any explicit mental reference to the
standard size of that kind of thing (PRICE, p. 65); but
though I need not have the standard size in mind,
reference to the kind of thing is inherent in any use of
"big" and "small".

Relational concepts in general raise difficulties of
which abstractionists are usually unaware—they
lump relations together with attributes as 'recurrent

characteristics' that we can recognize (*cf.* PRICE, p. 10). The trouble is that a relation neither exists nor can be observed apart from its converse relation; what is more, the concept of a relation and of its converse is one and the same indivisible mental capacity, and we cannot exercise this capacity without actually thinking of both relations together; *relativa sunt simul natura et intellectu.* It is difficult, in view of this, to give *any* account of our understanding the difference between "the knife is to the left of the book" and "the knife is to the right of the book". But I do not see how an abstractionist account of it is even possible; for all that is obtainable by abstraction, one would think, is ability to recognize the 'recurrent characteristic' of right-left ordering, not ability to tell which thing is to the left and which to the right. If we are to concentrate upon the 'recurrent characteristic', and 'abstract from' the terms between which the relations hold, what else can be the result? Yet surely it is only if there is at least an ability to tell which thing is to the right and which to the left, that we can say there exists a concept of *right and left*.

10

ABSTRACTIONISM AND COLOUR-CONCEPTS

THESE EXAMPLES so far show only that abstractionism does not cover the whole field of concepts. I wish to maintain a far stronger conclusion—that there is no concept at all of which an abstractionist account is adequate. If there were any truth in abstractionism, it would at any rate be adequate for concepts of simple sensible qualities, for concepts like *red* and *round*. Now if I possess the concept *red*, then I can perform acts of judgment expressible in sentences containing the word "red". This ability, however, certainly cannot be learned by any kind of attention to red patches for any length of time; even if after a course of attending to red patches the ability turned out to be present, we should still be justified in refusing to say it had been *learned* that way. We can say this quite as confidently as we can say that the ordinary use of the word "red" cannot be learned by hearing the word "red" uttered ceremonially in the presence of a red object—simply on this account, that such a ceremony is not the ordinary use of the word "red".

Price has the rare merit among abstractionists of having pointed out that ceremonious ostensive definition normally plays a rather small part in the learning of language. His own theory is that we learn the sense of words like "cat" and "black" by a double process of abstraction; that

the common feature, e.g. "cat", in these otherwise unlike utterances is gradually correlated with a common factor in observed environmental situations which are otherwise unlike. Similarly "black" gradually sorts itself out from another range of utterances which are otherwise unlike, and is correlated with a visible quality experienced in otherwise unlike situations. (PRICE, p. 215.)

This is much more plausible than the usual stuff about ostensive definition, but I think it is still open to two fatal objections. First, it is integral to the use of a general term that we are not confined to using it in situations including some object to which the term applies; we can use the terms "black" and "cat" in situations not including any black object or any cat. How could this part of the use be got by abstraction? And such use is part of the very beginnings of language; the child calls out "pot" in an 'environmental situation' in which the pot is conspicuous by its absence. Secondly, it is of course not enough, even when language is being used to describe the immediate situation, that we should utter a lot of words corresponding to several features of the situation; but the abstraction that Price appeals to could scarcely account for our doing anything more than this.

It is indeed hard to see at first sight what account other than an abstractionist account could possibly be given for such concepts as colour-concepts; and for this very reason such concepts are the abstractionists' favoured examples. The reason, surely, why men born blind cannot have colour-concepts is that they have no colour-sensations; and does not this imply that men who can see form their colour-concepts by attending to certain features given in their visual experiences?

In the first place, it is not true that men born blind can form no colour-concepts of any sort. A man born blind can use the word "red" with a considerable measure of intelligence; he can show a practical grasp of the logic of the word.[1] What is more, he may, if he

[1] "Red" has, for example, a very considerable logical resemblance to "hot"; both redness and heat admit of degrees, a surface can be red all over and hot all over, there can be redness or heat throughout a volume, etc., etc. A blind man could show that he had a concept of *red* akin to our own by using "red" and "hot" in logically similar ways; he need not be able to formulate the logical similarities.

is intelligent, grasp something of the aesthetic significance of red and its place in human life—like Locke's
blind man who said he thought scarlet must be like the
sound of a trumpet. Of course a man born blind cannot
have our colour-concepts; but this, it turns out, proves
nothing whatsoever. If it is logically impossible that a
man blind from birth should have colour-concepts
quite like those of a sighted man, then the unlikeness
cannot be regarded as a remarkable empirical fact,
throwing light upon the origin of concepts. Now concepts are mental capacities; somebody who is enabled
by his colour-concepts to do what somebody else cannot do has a specifically different capacity and thus a
different concept. A part of a sighted man's colour-
concepts is his ability to apply them to visual experiences; and a man blind from birth necessarily lacks
this ability. There is sufficient similarity between the
abilities of men blind from birth and of sighted men,
who alike use colour-words intelligently, for us to be
justified in speaking of "colour-concepts" in both
cases; what dissimilarity there is is a logical conse-
quence of the blind man's having always been blind,
and calls for no abstractionist explanation. If we supposed that men blind from birth could (logically) have
the same colour-concepts as sighted men, their not
having them would call for explanation; but such a
supposition would be just a muddle. Different men
may use tools that are quite similar in dissimilar ways;
but a concept is not externally related to its applications, as a tool is to its uses; a man who can do different things with his concept has a concept that is to
some extent different from the other fellow's.

   In point of fact, abstractionism goes to wreck even
over colour-concepts, as may be shown by a further

argument. Let us consider chromatic colour, i.e. colour other than white, grey, and black. The concept *chromatic colour*, in spite of my having had to explain the term by using a string of words, is surely no less 'simple', no less a concept of something 'given in direct experience', than the concept *red*. (One common meaning of the adjective "coloured" is the possession of chromatic colour—"coloured chalks", "coloured glass", "penny plain, twopence coloured".) Now it is quite impossible that I should form this concept, *chromatic colour*, by discriminative attention to a feature given in my visual experience. In looking at a red window-pane I have not two sensations, one of redness and one barely of chromatic colour; there are not, for that matter, two distinct sense-given features, one of them making my sensation to be barely a sensation of chromatic colour, the other making it a sensation of redness. If I abstract from what differentiates red from other chromatic colours I am abstracting from red itself; red is not chromatic colour *plus* a *differentia*, so that we can concentrate our attention upon chromatic colour and abstract from the *differentia*.

The difficulty I have just raised resembles one raised by Locke (*Essay*, III. iv. 6) about the relation between the concepts *red* and *colour*—"colour" having for him the wider sense of the word, covering also white, black, and grey. Locke observed that "red" cannot be defined by adding a *differentia* to "coloured", and inferred that the concept *coloured* cannot be reached by abstracting from the distinctive marks of the various colours. His solution is that the word "coloured" stands for 'the way' that all the 'ideas' of the several colours 'got into the mind'; "it signifies no more but such ideas as are produced in the mind only by the sight and have

entrance only through the eyes". Presumably his view
is that all 'ideas' with this common origin have a peculiar feel or look, which is manifest to 'inner sense' and
can be singled out abstractively; at least, I can think of
no other interpretation that makes his view plausible.
Even so, this is a pretty obvious makeshift. But I
would rather not discuss Locke's actual problem, because (using the word "colour" in his way) we should
encounter special, and for the moment irrelevant, difficulties about the concept *colour*. It is clear, however,
that the concept *chromatic colour* stands on the same
footing as the concept *red*, and does not raise any
of these peculiar difficulties; clear, too, that no such
account as Locke gives for the concept *colour* will fit.
Failing to account for so simple a concept as *chromatic
colour*, abstractionism must be pronounced finally
bankrupt.

11

MAKING CONCEPTS IS NOT A FINDING OF RECURRENT FEATURES

AT THIS POINT we feel inclined—indeed, almost
forced—to say that the mind makes a distinction
between redness and chromatic colour, although there
are not two distinct features to be found in the red
glass or in my visual sensation. And here, I think, we
are approaching the true solution.

"If the glass has not two distinct attributes, redness
and chromatic colour, how can these attributes be dis-

tinct anywhere? and then how can anything be chromatically coloured without being red?" This objection, natural as it is, rests upon a false Platonistic logic; an attribute is being thought of as an identifiable object. It would be better to follow Frege's example and compare attributes to mathematical functions.[1] "The square of" and "the double of" stand for distinct functions, and in general the square of x is different from the double of x; but if x is 2 then the square of x *is* the double of x, and the two are not in this case distinguishable even in thought. Similarly, since what is chromatically coloured is often not red, "the chromatic colour of x" or "x's being chromatically coloured" does not in general stand for the same thing as "the redness of x"; but if x is red, then it is by one and the same feature of x that x is made red and chromatically coloured; the two functions, so to speak, assume the same value for the argument x.

"If there are two distinct features to be found in my mental representation, and only one in the pane of glass, then my mind represents things otherwise than they are, i.e. represents them falsely. It would follow that the conceptual way of thinking distorts reality." How can we get over this difficulty?

The statement "An understanding which understands a thing otherwise than the thing is, is wrong" is ambiguous; the qualification of the verb "understands" by the adverb "otherwise" may relate either to the thing that is understood or to the person who understands. If it relates to the thing that is

[1] The use of this analogy does not commit us to the whole of Frege's apparatus. Readers who are interested in the development of the analogy may care to refer to my paper "Form and Existence" (*Proc. Arist. Soc.*, 1954–5).

D

understood, then the statement is true, its meaning being this: Any understanding that understands a thing *to be* otherwise than it is, is wrong. But this meaning is inapplicable to the case we are considering. For when our understanding frames a proposition about the colour of the glass, it does not assert that this colour is complex, but on the contrary that it is simple.—If, however, the qualification is taken to refer to the person who understands, then the statement is false; for the way it is with our understanding when we understand is different from the way it is with the thing we understand, in its actual existence. When our understanding understands things that are simple, it may understand them in its own complex fashion without understanding them *to be* complex.

The last paragraph is a translation from Aquinas (Ia q. 13 art. 12 ad 3 um), modified so as to fit my chosen example.[1] It appears to me to be a decisive solution to the problem of conceptual thought's 'falsifying' reality. We can now say something that goes for all concepts without exception: Having a concept never means being able to recognize some feature we have found in direct experience; the mind *makes* concepts, and this concept-formation and the subsequent use of the concepts formed never is a mere recognition or finding; but this does not in the least prevent us from applying concepts in our sense-experience and knowing sometimes that we apply them rightly. In all cases it is a matter of fitting a concept to my experience, not of picking out the feature I am interested in from among other features given simultaneously. Suppose I look at a lot of billiard balls on a table, and form the judgment that some of them are red and some are not. If I state

[1] For Aquinas's attitude to abstractionism, see the Appendix.

this judgment in words, "red" may plausibly be taken to report a feature of what I see, but "some" and "not" certainly cannot. But it would be perverse to infer that my distorting conceptual thought represents the reality as exhibiting features, somehood and nottishness, which are not really there; and no less perverse to argue that, since my judgment is correct, there must be somehood and nottishness *in rebus*. We must resist the perennial philosophical temptation to think that if a thought is to be true of reality, then it must copy it feature by feature, like a map. Even the use of the word "red" is not to be explained in terms of reporting or copying real features; for, as we saw, the terms "red" and "(chromatically) coloured" *may* answer to the same feature of the same thing; and again, what is logically distinctive in the use of colour-words is certainly not to be reached, by an act of abstraction, from the seeing of red things.

In rejecting abstractionism, we deny a privileged position to 'sensory' concepts, e.g. colour-concepts. These concepts are indeed specially involved in the procedure of describing one's sensations; geometrical concepts and colour-concepts enter into the description of visual sensations in a way that other concepts do not. If I look at a tomato, there is some justification for saying: "what I actually see can be *completely* described in terms of colour, shape, and size, without mentioning any other characteristics". There is however no reason to think that this gives 'sensory' concepts an epistemological primacy over others; for the description of sensations is a highly sophisticated exercise of concepts, and is secondary to the application of 'sensory' concepts to the material environment. In this primary, outward-looking application, 'sensory'

concepts have not in fact any privileged position; a child
with only a few concepts and only a small understanding of language may easily possess concepts like *door*
and *book* (and even the logical concept *other*, as in
"other hand", "other foot") before it has any colour-
concepts at all.

About psychological investigations designed to
prove that concepts are formed by abstraction, I think
it is safe to say that either what is studied is not the
formation of concepts, or it is manifest on a little consideration that the concepts were not formed by abstraction. The first criticism applies to such experiments
as getting rats to 'recognize triangles as such', i.e.
training them to react similarly to triangles of various
shapes and sizes. The psychologist may well say: "the
rats are able to perfect a type of behaviour which is
fully described by the implications in our use of the
term "concept" "; but 'our' (the experimenters') use of
the term is then wholly different from its use in this
book. (See HUMPHREY, p. 254.) This is not merely a
verbal point; the psychologist's explanation of such a
phrase as "the concept of triangularity" is what it is
now fashionable to call a persuasive definition, not
a mere Humpty-Dumpty pronunciamento. He can
scarcely deny that human beings show their possession
of the concept *triangle* by behaviour very different
from rats'; but he invites us to regard this difference as
unimportant.

Consider, on the other side, a study of genuine
concept-formation by Smoke (HUMPHREY, pp. 252–3,
275–6). On cards three inches square, figures of various
sorts were drawn; some of these were *pogs*, a *pog* being
a blue rectangle enclosing a blue circle that touches
only one long side of the rectangle. (Humphrey des-

cribes "*pog*" as a "nonsense name"; this is a self-contradictory expression, and is clearly wrong; "*pog*" is merely not part of ordinary language.) The subject was shown a number of *pogs*, was given the verbal instruction "Try to find out everything a figure must be if it is to be called a *pog*", and was told to raise his hand when he thought he knew what a *pog* was. His claim to knowledge was then tested by getting him to try (i) to pick out further *pogs*, (ii) to draw a *pog*, (iii) to define "*pog*" in words. Many subjects who failed at test (iii) succeeded at test (i). Humphrey thinks that this experiment shows "that a subject can form and utilize a concept without verbalization".

What Humphrey appears not to notice is that the verbal instruction given to the subject requires for its understanding some highly sophisticated concepts (the concept of *name*, the concept implicit in "everything that a thing must be if . . ."); such concepts are not among the first to be acquired, and the experiment does nothing to show that *they* are acquired 'without verbalization'. Again, the verbal instructions, and the whole set-up of the experiment, already delineate many of the logical peculiarities of the word "*pog*"; the word is not a mere nonsense-syllable at the start of the experiment (as Humphrey's tendentious term "nonsense name" suggests). "*Pog*" is to be a common noun, used to refer to a certain design of colours and shapes; a subject who has grasped this much already has an inchoate concept of a *pog*, and with one who had not grasped this much the experiment would not succeed. (The 'grasp' that I mean is a matter of partly knowing *how* to use the word "*pog*", not of knowing, explicitly judging, *that* the word is to be a common noun, etc.) So the experiment does not show that the subject can abstractively form the concept *pog* from scratch, independently of 'verbalization'.

Are we to say that subjects who can recognize *pogs* but cannot verbally define the term "*pog*" possess the concept *pog*? This certainly seems reasonable; how many of us could give a water-tight definition of "chair" or "money", words that we should certainly wish to say express concepts? Defining a term is normally a particular exercise of the corresponding concept rather than a way of getting the concept,[1] and performance of this exercise is not a necessary condition of having the concept. But though the subject may acquire the concept *pog* without being able to give a verbal definition of "*pog*", in the experimental set-up described the concept is acquired only against the background of a considerable command of language; to speak of 'forming concepts without verbalization' merely obscures the matter.

As I remarked before in reference to aphasia, I do not wish so to use the term "concept" that every concept necessarily involves some linguistic capacity. But Smoke's experiments certainly do not show that concepts can be formed *from scratch* by abstraction—by discriminative attention to features given in sense-experience—and that language is of no importance in their formation. Linguistic capacities, for an abstractionist, are necessarily an external, adventitious aspect of the possession of concepts. 'Fundamentally a concept is a recognitional capacity' for the abstractionist (PRICE, p. 355); so a depreciation of linguistic performances is an essential part of the abstractionist programme. Smoke has supplied no experimental support for such depreciation.

[1] As Aquinas already recognized: Ia q. 85 art. 2 ad 3 um.

12

RUSSELL'S THEORY OF JUDGMENT

WE MAY NOW RETURN to the analysis of the act of judgment, in which concepts are exercised. I shall begin by considering Russell's account of judgment (RUSSELL (1), (2), (3)).

(i) *The preambles to the act of judgment.* Russell starts from unexceptionable assertions: that we cannot judge if we do not know what we are judging about, and that we cannot understand the sentence in which a judgment is expressed unless we know the meanings of the several words. He then interprets "knowing the meaning of a word" as "standing in a direct cognitive relation to the thing that the word means". This 'direct cognitive relation' is called "acquaintance" and "awareness". When we know the meaning of a general term, we are acquainted with a universal entity that the general term signifies; awareness itself is one of the universal entities that we are aware of or acquainted with. As regards particular entities, we must not be misled by the fact that we understand proper names of people, and that we speak of "being acquainted" with them, into holding that people, or for that matter material things, can be objects of acquaintance. For Russell, only a man's sense-data and some psychical states of his own[1] can fall within his direct awareness; all other particular entities are known only by description. A grammatically proper

---

[1] Russell tentatively allows the possibility that the pronoun "I" (used as in the Cartesian "I think") also stands for an object with which the user is acquainted.

name is not logically so, but is short for a definite
description; and in order to understand a definite description I need only be acquainted with the universal
and particular entities that are meant by the terms
of the description—I need not be acquainted with
the thing described. (E.g. in order to understand the
definite description "the oldest of men" I need to be
acquainted with the universal entities that constitute
the meanings of "older than" and "man"; but I clearly
need not be acquainted even in the ordinary sense, still
less in Russell's, with the oldest of men.)

Russell's restricting our acquaintance to sense-data,
rather than material objects and other people, is partly
a matter of Cartesian doubt; I cannot doubt the existence of the sense-data, whereas I can doubt the existence of material objects and other people, so it is only
to the sense-data that I can stand in a 'direct cognitive
relation'. Another reason for the restriction is that
Russell regards the judgment as a complex, of which
the things *really* judged about (*sc.* the objects of
acquaintance) are actual constituents. Now if I judged
that the present King of France is fat and bald, it
would be hard to suppose that a bald fat man was
bodily a constituent of my judgment, even if my judgment were true and even if I had the honour to be
acquainted (in the ordinary sense) with the King.
Sense-data, on the other hand, are sufficiently private,
fleeting, and insubstantial to be plausibly taken as
constituents of a private mental act. As for the universal entities that are judged about, I do not think
their being constituents of judgments raises any worse
problems than their being constituents of any other particular entities (bad enough—*cf.* Plato's *Parmenides*).

(ii) *Analysis of the act of judgment.* Russell recants

his earlier view that when we judge we are acquainted with a single entity which, if the judgment were put into words, would be the meaning of the sentence expressing it. He holds that when James judges that *p*, there is an irreducible many-termed relation whose terms are, on the one hand, James's Cartesian ego, or at any rate some psychical element in James, and on the other hand those entities, universal and particular, with which James has to be acquainted in order to understand the sentence represented by "*p*". Let us take the simple case in which James judges that *a* is larger than *b*, *a* and *b* being objects of his awareness: the terms of the judging relation will then be: (1) a psychical element in James, *j*; (2) the object *a*; (3) the relation *larger than*; (4) the object *b*. We may symbolize the relation by "B (*j, a, larger than, b*)"; if we had instead "B (*j, b, larger than, a*)", this would mean that James judged that *b* was larger than *a*.

13

INADEQUACIES OF
RUSSELL'S THEORY

RUSSELL'S NOTION of our having direct acquaintance with universal entities is one which anybody who has been convinced by my argument that the formation of concepts is in no case a matter of *finding* something will be disposed to reject; and I shall not here discuss his notion of sense-data. Let us rather observe a peculiar twist of Russell's argument. He begins, I said, with the unexceptionable premise that in

order to understand a sentence you must understand
its several words; then he takes the meaning of a word
to be an object to which the user of the word has a
'direct cognitive relation'; then he forms his doctrine
about what sorts of entities we can stand in direct
cognitive relation to; then he notices that many words
in ordinary sentences do not have as their meanings
these sorts of entities; and then we are told that ordinary language is logically misleading, that ordinary
proper names are not logically such, etc., etc. But this
conclusion wrecks the inference with which the whole
theory began. For then knowing the meaning of a
word in ordinary language need not be acquaintance
(in Russell's sense) with an object that the word stands
for; and if it need not be, why should we suppose that
it ever is so?

Russell seems to me to be certainly right in denying
that the meaning of a sentence expressing James's
judgment is a complex object (or 'objective', as
Meinong would call it) with which James is acquainted.
Here we need to bring into play that 'sense of reality' to
which Russell rightly attaches importance in logical
investigations; we ought to find it incredible on the
face of it that if James believes something false, then
there is in the nature of things a falsehood that James
contemplates and, in his judgment, accepts. We may
indeed be disposed to attach some weight to this type
of argument: "Smith and James both judge that the
prisoner is guilty; so they both judge the same thing;
so there is a thing that they both judge". But whatever
force this argument has is only what it shares with the
argument: "Smith and James are both bald; so there is
a thing that they both are". If the common predicate
"bald" answers to something *in rebus*, so does the com-

mon predicate ". . . judges that the prisoner is guilty";
but this is no ground for supposing that a fragment of
the latter predicate, the *oratio obliqua* clause, has a
special sort of complex entity as its reference. Anyhow,
analysing judgments in terms of 'objectives' is a lazy
analysis; when judging is treated as a simple two-
termed relation, the complexity of the judgment is just
transferred in its entirety to that which is judged, the
'objective'.

Russell's positive account of the judging relation is
very sketchy, and it is easily shown that as it stands it
does not fulfil the logical conditions for an account of
judgment, given in §4. In particular, it does not show
how it is that we should be able to understand the
statement abbreviated as "James judges that p" provided that we understand both the expression "James
judges (that) . . ." and the sentence (whose *oratio
obliqua* form is) abbreviated to "p". If we use the
symbolism "B (j, a, R, b)" (*cf.* p. 47), where "R"
schematically represents a relation-word, then we can
give an analysis of "James judges that p" for all cases
in which "p" is interpreted as (the *oratio obliqua* form
of) a statement "aRb"; but this does not give us a clue
to the analysis in cases where "p" must bear a different
sort of interpretation; Russell's theory would here require different relations of judging (differing as to the
number and the logical types of the terms between
which they hold) for every different logical form of
sentences expressing judgments. This objection could
be overcome if we were given some recursive procedure
whereby the judging relations for more complex cases
could be defined in terms of those for simpler cases;
but in Russell there is no hint even of the need for such
a procedure, still less of its actual form.

Again, Russell holds that if James judges that *a* is larger than *b*, then the relation *larger than* is one of the things between which the judging relation obtains. But this idea, of a relation's being itself one among things that are related, is by no means clear. A relative term like "larger than" is incomplete; it carries with it, so to say, two blanks that need filling up ("—— is larger than ——"). The blanks need not, of course, be filled with singular terms: "some cat is larger than any rat" satisfies the requirement just as well as "Jemima is larger than Joey". Or again, the blanks may be filled up with variables, explicitly or implicitly; "*larger than* is converse to *smaller than*" is exponible as "for any *x* and any *y*, *x* is larger than *y* if and only if *y* is smaller than *x*". But how are the blanks to be filled up in "James judges that *a* is larger than *b*"? Russell would maintain that, logically speaking, "*a*" and "*b*" do not fill up what is lacking to the sense of "larger than"— *a*, *b*, and the relation *larger than* would on his view enter into the judging relation as separate terms, not as forming a complex on their own account. He holds this with some reason; he desires to give an account of false judgments without bringing in false 'objectives' as complexes composed of the entities judged about; and if *a*, *b*, and the relation *larger than* entered into the judging relation otherwise than as separate terms, it looks as though they might form such an objectionable complex. This feature of his theory was what I meant to suggest by separating the variables with commas in my notation "B (j, a, R, b)". But failing some specification how the double incompleteness of "larger than" is to be made good; failing some such development of "B $(j, a, larger than, b)$" as I gave just now for "*larger than* is converse to *smaller than*"; Russell's theory remains very obscure and unsatisfactory. Russell seems not to have noticed the difficulty.

A connected difficulty is this: since "*larger than*" is logically not to be read in "B (*j, a, larger than, b*)" as having its first blank filled up with "*a*" and its second with "*b*", how are we to distinguish this from "B (*j, b, larger than, a*)"? i.e. how are we to distinguish between "James judges that *a* is larger than *b*" and "James judges that *b* is larger than *a*"? Russell did notice this difficulty, but his attempts to deal with it are quite unavailing. To say that "the relation of judging places the constituents in a different order" (RUSSELL (1), p. 198) is no explanation, but just a way of stating the difference that has to be explained. In RUSSELL (2) on the other hand we read:

"the relation must not be abstractly before the mind, but must be before it as proceeding from *a* to *b* rather than from *b* to *a* . . . We may distinguish two 'senses' of a relation, according as it goes from *a* to *b* or from *b* to *a*. Then the relation as it enters into the judgment must have a 'sense' . . . Thus the judgment that two terms have a certain relation *R* is a relation of the mind to the two terms and the relation *R* with the appropriate sense" (pp. 183–4).

Yet if the relation *R* is before the mind, not as relating *a* and *b*, but only as a term of a judging relation that holds between the mind, *a*, the relation *R*, and *b*, how can there be any talk of the relation *R*'s 'proceeding' from *a* to *b* rather than from *b* to *a*? How can a relation that occurs not as relating things, but as one of the things related by another relation, occur with one or other 'sense'? This difficulty looks even worse if we consider how in fact the relation *R* does enter into the judgment, namely, as an object of thought. For not only is the concept of a pair of converse relations a single and indivisible mental capacity (*eadem est scientia oppositorum*); the exercise of that concept in judgment also brings in the two relations equally and simultaneously, for to judge that *a* bears the one relation to *b* is the very same act as judging that *b* bears the converse relation to *a*. Thus both relations of a pair of converses, or, in Russell's language, the relation *R* in both its 'senses', must enter into the act of judgment equally and simultaneously; his solution then collapses, and indeed the problem looks intractable.

14

A REVISION OF RUSSELL'S THEORY

A FORMALLY admissible solution will now be sketched. Its interpretation must for the moment be left aside; it is 'formally admissible' in the sense of avoiding the logical objections to Russell's theory.

We begin by introducing an operator "§( )"; if a relational expression is written between the brackets, we shall get a new relational expression of the same logical type as the original one. If "R" is dyadic, so is "§(R)"; if "R" is triadic, so is "§(R)"; and so on. In this respect the operator "§( )" resembles negation. Given any relational expression, we can form a negation of it, which will be a relational expression of the same polyadicity. But there is an important difference between the negation-operator and "§( )". Negation is what is called extensional; that is to say, if two relative terms "R" and "S" are truly applicable to precisely the same objects, then their negations also are applicable to precisely the same objects. But our analysis in terms of "§( )" would break down if we allowed the inference that when the relative terms "R" and "S" are applicable to just the same objects, then also the relative terms "§(R)" and "§(S)" are applicable to the same objects. Many logicians would object to introducing a non-extensional operator; but a plausible analysis of descriptions of judgments has not yet been given within a purely extensional logic.

We next introduce the term "idea", in an arbitrary and artificial sense; to distinguish this sense I shall write the word with a capital letter. In contemporary psychology "idea" is not in general use as a technical term, so there is no confusion with a competing technical sense to be feared; but it is well to guard against possible confusion with my own non-technical use of the word (as roughly equivalent to "view", "doctrine", "theory", etc.). By "an Idea" I shall mean the exercise of a concept in judgment; and I shall refer to particular Ideas in much the same way as I refer to the corresponding concepts; the exercise of James's concept *man* in a judgment will be an Idea of *man*. I deliberately leave this explanation vague and sketchy, because I do not want to commit myself to too many assumptions.

I shall speak hereafter of Ideas such as those of *every knife* and *some spoon*; this presupposes an understanding of the corresponding expressions "concept of *every knife*", "concept of *some spoon*". I wish to say that the concept *every knife* is exercised in any judgment to the effect that every knife is . . ., and is in fact the ability to frame judgments of this form; similarly, the concept *some spoon* is exercised in any judgment to the effect that some spoon is . . ., and is in fact the ability to frame judgments of this form. And exercises of these respective concepts in judgments will be Ideas of *every knife* and of *some spoon*.

My theory of judgment can now be stated. Suppose James judges that every knife is sharper than every spoon. This judgment comprises Ideas of *every knife* and of *every spoon*; let us call these two Ideas α and β respectively. My theory is that James's act of judgment consists of his Idea α, of *every knife*, standing in the relation §(sharper than) to his Idea β, of *every spoon*. This analysis gets over the difficulties about 'sense'; the difference between James's judging that every knife is sharper than every spoon and his judging that every spoon is sharper than every knife would be the difference between the Idea α's standing in the relation §(sharper than) to the Idea β and β's standing in that relation to α. We have also overcome another difficulty of Russell's theory—that we did not know how to extend it to (say) three-termed relations. A judgment to the effect that a three-termed relation R holds will consist in a man's having Ideas α, β, γ such that we have §(R)(α, β, γ); for "§(R)", like "R", will stand for a triadic relation, one therefore which can relate α, β, and γ.

In the dyadic case just discussed we may well suppose that

"α is James's Idea of *every knife*, and β is James's Idea of *every spoon*, and α stands in the relation §(sharper than) to β"

and: "α is James's Idea of *every knife*, and β is James's Idea of *every spoon*, and β stands in the relation §(blunter than) to α" are equivalent, mutually inferable, statements. This supposition seems to be demanded in order that we may say (as we surely must) that "James judges that every knife is sharper than every spoon" and "James judges that every spoon is blunter than every knife" are merely alternative descriptions of one and the same judgment. But can we consistently hold that in general (using the *Principia Mathematica* notation for "converse of") Cnv'§(R) and §(Cnv'R) are the same relation—e.g. that the converse of §(sharper than) is the relation §(blunter than)? We certainly need to distinguish between "James judges that some knife is sharper than any spoon" and "James judges that any spoon is blunter than some knife"; one might indeed hold that in judging the first thing James *eo ipso* judges the second thing, but the converse is not true. Thus we must also say of the two following statements made in terms of Ideas and §-relations:

"α is James's Idea of *some knife*, and β is James's Idea of *any spoon*, and α stands in the relation §(sharper than) to β",

"α is James's Idea of *some knife*, and β is James's Idea of *any spoon*, and β stands in the relation §(blunter than) to α",

that the second is implied by the first but not conversely. Accordingly, we must deny that the relations §(sharper than) and §(blunter than) are converse relations; and in general, even when the relation R is symmetrical, there will be a distinction between the relations Cnv '§(R) and §(Cnv'R).

A further example will show the power of my theory. Let α be, this time, James's Idea of [some Idea of *some knife*] and β James's Idea of [some Idea of *any spoon*];

and suppose that α stands in the relation §(§(sharper than)) to β. On my theory, these Ideas in this relation constitute James's judgment that some Idea of *some knife* stands in the relation §(sharper than) to some Idea of *any spoon*. Now since the relative terms formed with the operator "§(   )" were introduced to signify relations holding between Ideas in a single person's mind (viz. within a single act of judgment), we may well take this to be part of their sense; so "some Idea of *some knife* stands in the relation §(sharper than) to some Idea of *any spoon*" will be tantamount to saying "*somebody's* Idea of *some knife* stands in the relation §(sharper than) to *his own* Idea of *any spoon*". But this last is our analysis of "somebody judges that some knife is sharper than any spoon"; so α's standing in the relation §(§(sharper than)) to β will constitute a judgment on James's part *that somebody judges* that some knife is sharper than any spoon. This shows how our method can be extended to analysing reports of judgments to the effect that some judgment has occurred—reports involving a double *oratio obliqua* ("James judges that somebody judges that . . .").

Ability to account for such double *oratio obliqua* constructions is in any case a necessity for an adequate theory of judgments. For as soon as we understand the verb "to judge", the *oratio obliqua* construction, and the sense of the particular bit of *oratio obliqua* abbreviated to "*p*", we can understand "James judges that someone judges that *p*", "James judges that someone judges that James judges that *p*", and so on indefinitely (until sentences become too long for us to take in); and this surely involves that after the first stage we must have no new logical piece (so to speak) introduced into the game. My iterated use of the operator

"§(   )" certainly satisfies this condition. (To make my account of judgments about judgments tenable, it would also be necessary to assume, as I tacitly did, that given the sense of the term "Idea" and the virtual *oratio obliqua* construction, as we may call it, of "some knife" in "Idea of *some knife*", we have all that we need in order to understand the double virtual *oratio obliqua* in "Idea of [some Idea of *some knife*]". For if this were not so, we should get something 'logically new' introduced; which, as I have said, would disqualify our analysis.)

It may be objected that the following two statements certainly cannot be treated as equivalent, even though, according to our theory, the sentence from which they are obtained by prefixing "James judges that . . ." would be equivalent:

A. "James judges that somebody judges that some knife is sharper than any spoon";

B. "James judges that somebody's Idea *some knife* stands in the relation §(sharper than) to that person's Idea *any spoon*".

How could B be true unless, not only were A true, but also James had accepted Geach's analysis of judgments? B, then, cannot be equivalent to A; so our analysis of double *oratio obliqua* in reports of judgments seem to break down.

But suppose instead of A I had written:

A'. "James judges that somebody judges that some knife stands in the relation *sharper than* to any spoon".

Are A and A' equivalent? Does the truth of A' require, over and above the truth of A, that James shall have done some philosophizing about relations? Not at all; my writing down A' instead of A would make no difference

to the statement I made, it would merely display my
own familiarity with a bit of philosophical jargon.
The relation between A and B is, I think, similar;
though B, unlike A , is not just a pedantic circum-
locution for A. If James expresses his judgment in the
sentence "somebody judges that some knife is sharper
than any spoon", *eo ipso* James is in fact relating the
phrases "some knife" and "any spoon" to the realm of
what *I* call Ideas, and taking "sharper than" to stand
not for the relation it ordinarily stands for, but for the
relation that *I* express by "§(sharper than)"; he understands the words "some knife", "any spoon", "sharper
than", in a special *oratio obliqua* sense—in their *un-
gerade Sinn*, as Frege would say. But this understanding is a matter of 'knowing how' rather than 'knowing
that'; it comes out in James's practical mastery of the
oratio obliqua construction, not in his ability (if he has
any) to give a philosophical account of that construction. When I, on the other hand, am concerned to
bring out the logical force of James's judgment, it is
open to me to use logical devices and terms of my own
invention, regardless of whether James would understand them.

In RUSSELL (3) there is an argument against the
view that judgments comprise ideas; the vague word
"idea" is here used by Russell in very much the same
way as I use "Idea", and his arguments, if correct,
would go against my present theory, so I shall take the
liberty of writing "Idea" for his "idea" throughout.—
Russell holds that the view that a judgment is built up
out of Ideas probably depends on a failure to reach a
correct theory of descriptions. There is a popular use of
"idea" in which "my idea of Julius Caesar" means
much the same as "what I know about Julius Caesar".

"what I take to hold true of Julius Caesar". In this
sense, Russell would allow some truth to the statement
that in order to make a judgment about Julius Caesar
I must first have an idea of Julius Caesar; for Russell
admits, he is in fact actually contending, that 'in order
to discover what is actually in my mind when I judge
about Julius Caesar, we must substitute for the proper
name a description made up of some of the things that
I know about him'. This certainly shows that Julius
Caesar himself does not enter bodily into my judgment
as a constituent; but it does not show that in his stead
there does enter some Idea. The description that expresses how I think of Julius Caesar could be so
phrased as to contain only words for entities (universal
and particular) that are objects of my awareness; and
these entities, Russell thinks, which are 'the actual
objects concerning which we judge', do enter as constituents into the judgment-complex; no need to postulate any Ideas that shall go proxy for them.

Secondly, Russell objects that if in an act of judgment there are included Ideas of what we are judging
about, then 'Ideas become a veil between us and outside things—we never really, in knowledge, attain to
the things we are supposed to be knowing about, but
only to the Ideas of these things'. Surely it is preferable
to hold that there is a mental constituent which stands
in the two-termed relation of awareness to the several
things that are judged about, and also stands in the
irreducibly many-termed relation of judgment to all of
them together? Is not the appeal to Ideas just due to a
lingering prejudice against relations, so that an Idea
'in' the mind seems preferable to a relation 'between'
the mind and other things?

Russell's talk of 'complexes' and 'constituents'

embodies, I think, a radical confusion. If a word for x is part of a description of y, it does not follow that x is a constituent of y; "Denmark" is a part of "the capital of Denmark", but Denmark is not a part or constituent of the capital of Denmark. So there is no reason why a thing that is judged about should be a constituent of my act of judgment, merely because the description of the act mentions the thing. Sense-data and universals may appear better candidates for the position of elements in my act of judgment than a man who died two thousand years ago; but there is no better reason in logic why they should be elements or constituents of it.

The argument that if our judgment contains Ideas of things, not the things themselves, then what we judge about is the Ideas, not the things, is a sophism frequently used by idealists; Russell's use of it (of course to prove an anti-idealist conclusion) may well be a hangover from his idealist beginnings. One might as well argue that all disputes are about words, because they are conducted in words. If Ideas are part of our judging about things, it does not follow that Ideas are what we are really judging about; no more than words which are part of our talk are what we are really talking about.

I do not think, then, that there is anything in Russell's objection to Ideas. And my own recourse to Ideas in the analysis of judgment certainly involves no reluctance to bring relations into the account.

15

JUDGMENTS ABOUT SENSIBLE
PARTICULARS

THE CONTENT of the judgments considered in the last section was wholly universal or general; a verbal expression of such a judgment would contain no demonstratives and no proper names. This stands in marked contrast with Russell's examples: judgments that Desdemona loves Cassio, that Charles I died in his bed (or: on the scaffold), that the Sun is shining, that Bismarck was an astute diplomatist, that Scott was the author of *Waverley*; and again, judgments that *this* is yellow, that *this* is before *that*, that I am acquainted with A (where "*this*", "*that*", and "A" are given unique reference by someone's direct experience). (RUSSELL (1), (2), (3).) In point of fact, Russell only attempts to analyse the second sort of judgment, which relates, not merely to singular objects, but to objects of direct acquaintance. His treatment of the other sort of judgment, which is expressed by using ordinary proper names like "Bismarck" and "the Sun", is entirely unsatisfactory. Sometimes we find such objects as human beings treated as constituents of the judgments in whose expression their proper names occur—a procedure quite inconsistent with Russell's general view. No doubt this is done in order to get simple, familiar, illustrations; Russell makes believe that the proper names stand for judgment-constituents, i.e. objects of acquaintance that are being judged about, although on his own showing this is never true. Sometimes, on the other hand, in discussing

61

such examples Russell is expressly concerned to bring out their concealed logical form: when I say "Bismarck is an astute diplomatist", my use of the word "Bismarck" takes the place of some description, and I am using in my judgment what this description would mean. What I really judge is (say) that *the first Chancellor of the German Empire was an astute diplomatist*; and by Russell's theory of descriptions the italicized words would mean something like: "there was somebody who was a Chancellor of the German Empire, before whom nobody was a Chancellor of the German Empire, and who was an astute diplomatist". But now the trail is lost; for Russell makes no attempt (in RUSSELL (1), (2), (3)) to deal with judgments whose verbal expression would even approach the complexity of the sentence just quoted. Russell's theory of descriptions enables us to analyse a sentence containing a definite description, only so long as that description does not occur in *oratio obliqua*. For although, if Russell is right, we may pass from "James judges that he who shot Lincoln shot himself" to "James judges that somebody shot Lincoln and shot himself and that no two (different) people shot Lincoln", this latter statement is not, on Russell's principles, a finally satisfactory analysis; for it still presents the appearance of asserting a two-termed judging relation—the contents of the "that"-clause are not split up, so as to reveal the real polyadicity of the special judging relation here involved, and we have no indication how to do this.

Thus Russell only deals with singular judgments, and only with those singular judgments which relate to objects of direct acquaintance. I think this is a further reason for saying that an attempt to explain judgments on his lines is likely to fail. There is much more hope that an account designedly adequate for general judgments will turn out adaptable to singular judgments, than there is of the reverse adaptation, to which Russell would be committed; and we find no hint (in RUSSELL (1), (2), (3)) how his theory could be adapted to fit general judgments.

If we reject as spurious his examples of judgments expressible with proper names, Russell actually analyses only such judgments as that *this* is red or that *this* is before *that*. But are the expressions "this is red", "this is before that", genuine expressions of any actual human judgment? Is not a genuine expression of judgment something more like "that flash was before this bang"? Russell might reply that this last statement is analysable as: "*that* is a flash, and *this* is a bang, and *that* is before *this*". I propose, however, to ignore this analysis and attack the problem another way. How, I shall ask, is a judgment expressible as "that flash was before this bang", which refers to a particular flash and a particular bang, to be distinguished from a judgment, with the same verbal expression, which refers to another flash and another bang? What constitutes this reference to definite particulars? Or again, what is the difference between "there are white cats", "some cats are white", on the one hand, and on the other hand "these cats are white"? How do the judgments they express differ? What constitutes the reference to a particular set of cats?

In all such cases, I should maintain, there is no difference to be found on the side of the judgment itself. What we may call the intelligible content of the judgment is the same in all judgments expressible as "that flash was before this bang", regardless of which flash and bang are in question. (In terms of the analysis in §14, there would always in such cases be an Idea *flash* standing in the relation §(before) to an Idea *bang*. But what I now say does not stand or fall with this analysis.) We may see how the special reference to *that* flash and *this* bang comes in, if we ask ourselves the question: How could the utterance "flash before bang" be taken to refer to a particular flash and bang? The answer is obvious; the utterance can be, and probably will be, so understood in a sensory context in which the hearer notices a flash and a bang. Similarly, the utterance "some cats, white" could be taken to refer to particular cats if its hearer was looking attentively in the right direction. The content of the judgment is always intelligible and conceptual—acquaintance with a particular sensible thing is no part of the judgment itself—but an act of judgment performed in a particular sensory context may thereby be referred to particular sensible things. It is clear, indeed, that the act of judgment must bear a closer relation than mere simultaneity to the context of sense-perception that gives it its special reference to *these* particular sensible things; I am not prepared to characterize this special relation it must bear to its context. (So far as I can see, it is quite useless to say the relevant sense-perceptions must be being attended to; either this does not give a sufficient condition, or else "attended to" is a mere word for the very relation of judgment to sense-perception that requires analysis—"James judges, attending to such-and-such sense-perceptions" meaning no more than that his judgment *refers to* what he thus perceives.) But I do not think this throws any doubt upon what I have said; although more remains to be said.

The problem I have just been discussing—how we judge about sensible particulars—was much agitated in the Middle Ages; and in my solution of it I believe I am following Aquinas. Aquinas's expression for the relation of the 'intellectual' act of judgment to the context of sense-perception that gives it a particular reference was "*conversio ad phantasmata*", "turning round towards the sense-appearances". This metaphorical term is obviously a mere label, with negligible explanatory value; but it does not pretend to be more than a label. Aquinas has, in my opinion, at least rightly located the problem; the problem is not how we advance from judgments like *this is before that* to more general judgments, but contrariwise how a judgment inherently general can be tied down to referring to particular things (Ia q. 86 art. 1).

Quite similar considerations apply to judgments involving tense. The difference between judgments to the effect that a hydrogen bomb *will be* exploded and that a hydrogen bomb *has been* exploded is an intelligible or conceptual difference—a specifically different exercise of concepts is involved. But there is no conceptual difference between judgments formed in different years to the effect that.a hydrogen bomb has been exploded, although such a judgment formed in 1940 would have been false and one formed in 1956 would be true. The difference between the two judgments is constituted by their standing in relation to different sensory contexts (by there being a different *conversio ad phantasmata*—AQUINAS, Ia q. 85 art. 5 ad 2 um); but it is a great mistake to try to bring in these contexts into any setting forth of that which is judged (a mistake very frequently committed—*cf.* the articles

on tensed statements that have appeared, e.g. in
Analysis of recent years[1]).

16

JUDGMENTS INVOLVING IDENTIFICATIONS

JUDGMENTS expressed by using proper names
present a much more difficult problem than is
raised by demonstratives and tenses. What I have to
say is meant to rule out solutions that seem to me
clearly wrong, rather than to offer a positive solution. There are two statements about proper names
that have become widely accepted slogans: first, that
proper names are disguised (definite) descriptions;
secondly, that proper names have no connotation at
all. At any rate these slogans cannot both be true; my
own view is that they are both entirely false. It is
anyhow important to examine them, because on the
truth of the matter there will depend what we ought
to say about judgments expressed by means of proper
names.

The theory that proper names are disguised definite
descriptions was first devised by Russell (*cf.* RUSSELL
(3)) and has since been maintained in an even more
intransigent form by Quine (in QUINE (1) and other
works). From a psychological point of view it is
palpably false; when I refer to a person by a proper
name, I need not either think of him explicitly in a
form expressible by a definite description, or even be

[1] Some of these have been reprinted in the volume *Philosophy and
Analysis*, ed. Margaret Macdonald (Blackwell, 1954).

prepared to supply such a description on demand (not, that is, with any confidence that the description really is exclusive). Quine, however, has made a strenuous attempt to get over the difficulty. "We may insist", he says,

"that what are learned by ostension, or direct confrontation, be never names but solely predicates. This we may insist upon at the level strictly of logical grammar, without prejudice to epistemology . . . because we grant the epistemologist any of the words which he traces to ostension; we merely parse them differently. Instead of treating the ostensively learned word as a *name of* the shown object to begin with, we treat it to begin with as a predicate *true* exclusively of the shown object; then we construe the name, as such, as amounting to "$(\imath x)Fx$" where "F" represents that primitive predicate[1] . . . Given any singular term of ordinary language, say "Socrates" or "Cerberus" . . . the proper choice of "F" for translation of the term into "$(\imath x)Fx$" need in practice never detain us";

Quine is prepared to allow such 'predicates' as "is-Socrates" and "is-Cerberus" as interpretations of the predicate-letter "F", "since any less lame version", he says, "would, if admissible as a translation at all, differ at most in expository value and not in meaning". (QUINE (1), pp. 218–19.)

Now suppose somebody chooses to call her dog "Cerberus", and introduces him under that name: "this is Cerberus". A follower of Quine 'insists' on parsing "Cerberus" as a predicate. Later on, he says

[1] "$(\imath x)Fx$" is to be read "*the* thing that is F", "F" representing a logical predicate.

of another dog: "here is another Cerberus". On Quine's
view, this would be merely a factual mistake, which
the owner could suitably correct by saying "No, there's
only one Cerberus". Would it not then be in place to
ask the owner how she knows there is only one Cerberus? and is not this plainly a silly question, in fact?
As the owner intended "Cerberus" to be used, such
expressions as "here is another Cerberus" or "there are
several Cerberuses" are not just false statements—they
are excluded altogether as moves in the language-
game played with "Cerberus". The owner did not,
then, mean "Cerberus" as a predicate; and it is useless
to 'insist that it be' one—this 'insistence' is insistence
on playing a different game with the word, and is
irrelevant to the owner's use of it.—Of course there
are grammatically proper names that can be con-
strued as disguised definite descriptions: e.g. "Homer"
as "the man who composed both the Iliad and the
Odyssey". But these are altogether exceptional.

The theory that proper names have no connotation
historically forms part of a highly muddled logical
doctrine about 'connotation and denotation'. A clearer
way of stating it is to be found in Locke: that there is
nothing essential to an individual. To a thing to which
a general term is rightly applied, those attributes may
be said to be essential which logically follow from the
general term's being true of it; but no attributes logically follow from a thing's being given a proper name.
(*Essay*, III. vi. 4.) Notice that I spoke of 'rightly'
applying a general term, but not of 'rightly' giving a
thing a proper name; for, on the theory I am considering, we give proper names by fiat and there is no right
or wrong about the procedure. A thing is introduced
to me by its proper name, and thereafter I can refer to

the same thing by using that name; but the name tells one nothing about the attributes of the thing.

The sense of a proper name certainly does not involve anything about the peculiarities of the individual so named, which distinguish it from other individuals of the kind; a baby, a youth, an adult, and an old man may be unrecognizably different, although the same name is borne throughout life. But it is meaningless to say without qualification that the baby, the youth, the adult, and the old man are 'the same', or 'the same thing', and that this is what justifies us in calling them by the same name; nor yet is it a matter for our free decision whether or not they are to be deemed 'the same'. "The same" is a fragmentary expression, and has no significance unless we say or mean "the same X", where "X" represents a general term (what Frege calls a *Begriffswort* or *Begriffsausdruck*). What is implied by our use of the same name throughout a period of years is that the baby, the youth, the adult, and the old man are one and the same *man*. In general, if an individual is presented to me by a proper name, I cannot learn the use of the proper name without being able to apply some *criterion* of identity; and since the identity of a thing always consists in its being the same X, e.g. the same *man*, and there is no such thing as being just 'the same', my application of the proper name is justified only if (e.g.) its meaning includes its being applicable to a *man* and I keep on applying it to one and the same *man*.

On this account of proper names, there *can* be a right and wrong about the use of proper names. Suppose that an astronomer observes two different fixed stars at two different times, erroneously believes that one and the same planet has been observed on both occasions, and christens this supposed planet "Vulcan". His use of the word would be justified if he had succeeded in identifying an astronomical object as *one and the same planet* on different occasions; and since in point of fact his identification was a mistake, his use of the term "Vulcan" was also a mistake; he has given the term no reference, no use, whatsoever, and there is nothing he can do except to drop it. A similar situation arose in a detective story I once read (*The Wraith*, by Philip MacDonald). The man suspected of murder was one A. G. Host; but the great detective discovered that two men had on different occasions acted the part of Host; so that the identification of *one and the same man* as the person who had done various things, which was expressed by using the proper name "A. G. Host", was misconceived. After this discovery, people who knew the facts could clearly no longer use "A. G. Host" as a proper name.

It has often been argued that it cannot be part of the meaning of a proper name that its bearer should be a man, because we cannot tell this just by hearing the name, and because there is nothing to stop us from giving the same name to a dog or a mountain. You might as well argue that it cannot be part of the meaning of "beetle" that what it is applied to must be an insect, because we cannot learn this meaning just from the sound of the word, and because "beetle" is also used for a sort of mallet. In a given context, the sense of "beetle" does include: being an insect, and the sense of "Churchill" does include: being a man.

Again, my view of proper names does not commit me to an Aristotelian doctrine about 'essences'. I hold, indeed, that the sense of "Churchill" does include: being one and the same man (*homo*), and the term "man" ("*homo*") is traditionally assigned to the category of substance; but similarly I hold that the terms "Venus" and "Thames" have as part of their respective senses: being one and the same planet, and being one and the same river. Now a defender of substance would not, I think, wish to regard either "planet" or "river" as a word for a kind of substance; a planet would be an aggregate of substances of many kinds, and the identity of a river is not identity of the substance (the water) that occupies the river-bed. My thesis is that for any proper name there is some interpretation of "X" such that we can truly say "the continued application of this proper name requires, as part of the sense of the name, that it be always applied to the same X ". But the general term represented by "X" need not stand for a kind of substance, even if we allow a distinct category of terms that do so. My thesis relates only to 'nominal essence', and has nothing to do with 'real essences'.

It follows from this account of proper names that from a statement in which a proper name is used— "Smith committed seven burglaries, then Smith committed a murder, then Smith was hanged"—we can distil out a statement in purely general terms—"*a man* committed seven burglaries; then *the same man* committed a murder, and was then hanged". I should also hold that this is *all* the intelligible content that can be got out of the statement, since I hold that the sense of a proper name never includes anything about the individual peculiarities of its bearer. (Sometimes I may expressly advert in my mind to other people's using the name "Smith" for the man who had all these adventures: "a man known to others as "Smith" committed seven burglaries (etc.)". But this is not

F

necessary—no more necessary than that I should think of a cow always as an animal that other people call "a cow".) Thus on my view there is no intrinsic difference between a judgment that Smith had a certain series of adventures, and a judgment that some one man successively had the adventures (or perhaps: that some one of the men called "Smith" did so); there is nothing within the act of judgment itself to point to *the right* Smith. 'If God had looked into our minds, he would not have been able to see *there* whom we were speaking of' (WITTGENSTEIN, Part II, p. 217; my italics).

So far, what I have said about judgments expressed by means of proper names is like what I said about those expressed with demonstrative pronouns; and in this case too the singular judgment would have the same content as one statable in purely general terms. (As before, judgments' having the same content would be analysable, on the view I developed in the last Section but one, as their consisting of similar sets of Ideas, related by the same §-relations.) But we cannot in our present case appeal to *conversio ad phantasmata* as what makes a judgment relate to the right Smith. We could explain the particular reference of judgments expressed with demonstrative pronouns by relating them to an immediate sensory context; but of course we can talk about Smith and make judgments about him when he is not present to our senses. We might try relating the judgment to mental images of one sort or another (which would likewise be *phantasmata* for Aquinas): e.g. to memory-images of Smith's appearance or of his name. But my visual image of how Smith looked may be very inadequate, and may be known by me to be so; and very many people have the name "Smith". So in general the mind will not contain anything uniquely relating to Smith—an unmistakable photograph or relic of him, so to say. So far as I can see, a description of the judgment as relating to the right Smith is possible only if it places the judgment in a real-life context described as including that Smith. The problem how you call Smith, the right Smith, to mind is like the problem how you *call* him (WITTGENSTEIN, Part I, §691). Although lots of people are called "Smith", the summons "Smith!" may be quite effective to fetch the Smith I want if he is the only man of that name within earshot; and similarly, a judgment that might in principle relate to many men may yet in a particular real-life context be relatable to just one.

The problem how I can continue to refer to a man *as* the same man over a period of time is a matter of my own mental acts; my identification may be mistaken, but I should none the less be thinking *as it were* of the same man; and if the identification is mistaken, then we can give no account of it by describing a context that includes the man I was all along judging about, since there will have been no such man. Such identification is essentially appealed to in my account of proper names; in a series of statements about Smith, I hold, "Smith" could be replaced the first time by "a man", and in later occurrences by "the same man" or "the man" or "he". Now from a logical point of view the string of statements thus obtained, with the name "Smith" eliminated, are just one long existentially quantified statement; "for some x, x was a man, and x committed seven burglaries, and x committed a murder, and x was hanged". But this would clearly not do as an account of how judgments are actually formed—especially if the one long statement would have to be *very* long, as may easily happen when I keep on learning things about somebody.

Let us consider a clear case of the problem, uncomplicated by proper names. I say first of all "There's a man on the quarry-edge"; five minutes later I say "Now he's gone—he must have fallen in!" The identification expressed by my use of "he" cannot be explained by bringing the man himself into the story; perhaps I was wrong and there never was a man on the quarry-edge. My use of "he" in this case has nothing to do with *conversio ad phantasmata*; "he" does not get its meaning from anything that could be sensibly indicated. Crudely: "he" does not mean "the man I am now looking at, or pointing to" but "the man I *meant* a little while ago"; what is required in my referring to him as "he" is not a present *sense-perception* but a recent *thought*. (To use Aquinas's language: the pointing, *demonstratio*, effected by the demonstrative word "he" is not *ad sensum* but *ad intellectum*.) Although my later judgment need not be held to incorporate my earlier one (which, I argued, it would be very unplausible to hold if there were a long series of judgments all relating as it were to the same person); nevertheless there must be an intelligible difference of content between my actual pair of judgments five minutes apart, and a pair of successive judgments that *a* man is on the brink of the quarry and that *a* man (not necessarily the same nor necessarily a different one) has fallen in. There must be some special relation of the two judgments in the former case; but I am at present unable to say more than this.

17

ANALOGY THEORIES OF
PSYCHOLOGICAL CONCEPTS

I NOW TURN to a theory of judgment *prima facie* very different from the one sketched in §14. As I remarked in §4, there are many languages in which, as in English, the only difference between the statements "James said that *p*" and "James judged that *p*" is that they have different main verbs. The theory I am now going to discuss takes this as its clue to the nature of judgment; the concept *judging* is viewed as an analogical extension of the concept *saying*. I must begin, then, with some general remarks about the 'analogy' theory of psychological concepts. This theory is *not* to be supported by appealing to the etymology of words for mental acts. Such etymologies are often very obscure (e.g. that of "credere", "to believe", in Latin) and often have no apparent relevance when they are clear (what has *standing under* to do with *understanding*?). Again we must distinguish between what may be called *casual* and *systematic* analogies. In casual analogies, a particular epithet may be suggestive or even 'inevitable' in its metaphorical use, but this gives us no indication for the transferred use of another epithet of the same family; an understanding of "yellow—that's the only word for him!" does not give us a clue as to what would be meant if another colour-word were substituted for "yellow". The sort of analogy that is important is that in which a whole system of description is transferred to an analogical use; the *oratio obliqua* construction, for example, whose

primary use is to report actual speech, is transferred to
describing the content of judgments.

What is the meaning of calling a description of a
mental act "analogical" or "metaphorical", except by
contrast with a literal description? and if the literal
description is available, how can the analogy be of any
importance for the concept of the mental act? This
objection to the expression "analogy" or "metaphor"
is easily got over. What makes the description to be
analogical is not that there is a literal description of
the mental act, to replace the metaphor, but that there
is another application of the description, and of the
whole system of description to which it belongs; an
application that may be called literal, in contrast to
the transferred application to mental acts. We may
agree that if a metaphorical description of a mental act
is replaceable by a non-metaphorical description of
that very act, then the metaphor can have little importance for the concept of that sort of act.

Someone may, however, argue thus: "Even if in our
actual language there is no way of replacing a metaphor used to describe a mental act (except perhaps by
another metaphor), this can only be an accident of
language. For, in order to see that the metaphorical
system of description is appropriate to the facts it is
used to describe, we must already be able to discern
those characteristics of mental acts which make the
description appropriate. Now the characteristics (for
example) of a judgment that is described by a transferred use of the *oratio obliqua* construction will be
characteristics not to be found in the pieces of language
that this construction is primarily used to report; so a
concept of the mental characteristics must be an
entirely new concept, which it is merely misleading to

call an 'analogical' extension of the concept exercised in the primary use of *oratio obliqua*. And if we can discern, and form a concept of, these mental characteristics on their own account, then we could if we chose invent a special word, which would be used *only* to express our exercise of the new psychological concept. So the analogy of mental judgments to actually uttered statements cannot be an indispensable part of our concept *judgment*; and in general psychological concepts cannot be irreducibly analogous in character."

If forming a concept consisted in extracting a repetitive feature from our experience and becoming able to recognize its recurrences, then indeed psychological concepts extracted from 'inner sense' would be in no way dependent on the analogies afforded by other concepts extracted from sense-experience; only when we already possessed the psychological concepts could we go on to observe the appropriateness of such analogies. I have argued, however, that no concept whatsoever is to be identified with a recognitional capacity. In all cases it is a matter of fitting my concept to my experience—of exercising the appropriate concept—not of picking out the feature I am interested in from among others simultaneously given in experience. Now exercise of a particular set of concepts in a particular way (e.g. the exercise involved in describing something by means of a particular set of words in the *oratio obliqua* construction) may be appropriate both as applied to A and as applied to B, although A is not 'like' B; and we may perfectly well know its appropriateness in both cases (in the 'knowing-how' sense; that is to say, we may know when to exercise our concepts thus, whether or not we can formulate to ourselves a rule as to when we ought to do so).

On our theory of concepts, there is no reason that can be offered in advance why psychological concepts, or some of them, should not be irreducibly analogous. It might very well be that we always get the know-how of a particular set of concepts first of all in application to sensible things (e.g. human utterances), and then in psychological applications. Any alleged example of this would have to be investigated on its own account before we could decide about its genuineness. On the other hand, our theory destroys the old grounds for saying that psychological concepts *must* be irreducibly analogous. Somebody who held abstractionist views, and at the same time held that sense-experience offered all the material we have for performing abstraction upon—a combination of views expressed in the old maxim "*Nihil in intellectu nisi prius in sensu*" —would be obliged to maintain that we first extract concepts from sense-experience and then give them an extended psychological use; his position would, in my opinion, both involve very unplausible accounts of certain psychological concepts, and be extremely hard to maintain on an abstractionist footing. Our rejection of abstractionism means that we are not antecedently committed either way as to the analogousness of a given psychological concept.

It is a mere matter of terminology whether we say that the psychological concept is a new concept derived by 'analogy' from a previous concept, or that we exercise an old concept in new, psychological applications 'analogous' to our former exercise of it. A concept is a capacity for certain exercises of the mind; and as regards capacities generally, if a man formerly

capable of certain performances in one domain comes
to perform similarly in another domain, it is quite
arbitrary whether we say that his former capacity now
extends to a new domain of exercise or that he has
acquired a new capacity closely related to his old one.
I shall say indifferently "analogical concepts" and
"analogous exercises of concepts".

18

PSYCHOLOGICAL USES OF *ORATIO RECTA*

ONE OF THE MOST convincing analogy-theories
of psychological concepts is the view that modes
of description primarily applied to actual bits of
written and spoken language are transferable to the
role of describing the content of judgments—that
which is judged. As I have remarked, in many languages the same *oratio obliqua* construction is used to
report a man's words and to report his thoughts. But
I would rather not appeal to this fact in my discussion
of the 'interior language' analogy. For one thing, the
logic and grammar of *oratio obliqua* clauses involve a
lot of complications, mostly trivial. What is worse,
there is a plausible argument to show that it involves
a vicious circle to treat the use of *oratio obliqua* in
describing actual bits of language as being logically
prior to psychological uses of the construction. *Oratio
obliqua* serves to give us, not the actual words that
somebody said, but rather their gist or purport; but
does not this term "purport" smuggle in a psychological concept? Should we not say that *oratio obliqua*

serves to tell us what the speaker had in mind, or what
he wanted to evoke in his hearers' minds? If so, "James
said that p", so far from being logically prior to "James
had it in mind that p" and other such psychological
expressions, needs to be analysed in terms of them. I
think this objection could be answered, but it would
take us too far round to do so directly; instead of this
I shall turn from *oratio obliqua* to *oratio recta*, actual
quotation. The primary role of *oratio recta* is certainly
not psychological; it serves to report what somebody
actually said or wrote. But *oratio recta* can be used
metaphorically to report what somebody thought,
'said in his heart' (without, of course, implying that
the thinker had the quoted words in his mind); such
constructions are frequent in the Authorized Version
of the Bible: "The fool hath said in his heart "There is
no God" "; "They said in their heart "Let us destroy
them together" ".[1] Clearly we could *always* describe
judgments by using *oratio recta* in this way; *oratio
obliqua* is logically superfluous. (Certain arguments
that have been advanced against the replacement of
oratio obliqua by *oratio recta* will be answered in §18.)
And here we have a clear case of a linguistic device
whose psychological application is logically secondary
to its application to sensible things—bits of actual
written and spoken language. In order to understand
how this device works, we shall have to discuss in some
detail the logic of *oratio recta* in its primary or literal
application.

In contemporary logic there is a pretty general recognition of the rule that when we write down an
expression for the purpose of talking about that very

[1] The Authorized Version of the Bible does not use quotation
marks; I have here adapted the texts to my own practice.

expression, we must show what we are doing by enclosing that expression within quotes; if this rule is not
strictly observed, actual fallacies are likely to arise.
Nothing in spoken language corresponds to this use
of quotation-marks; the beginnings of the sentences
"man is an animal" and " "man" is a noun" are
phonetically quite alike. There is indeed a particular
tone of voice that is conventionally represented by
using quotes, as in "He introduced me to his 'wife' ";
but such quotes (which are sometimes called "scare-
quotes") are of course quite different from quotes used
to show that we are talking about the expression they
enclose. In this work I have tried to follow a strict rule
of using single quotes as scare-quotes, and double
quotes for when I am actually talking about the expressions quoted.[1] I shall distinguish between a *quotation* and a *quoted expression*; the quoted expression is
what stands between quotes, e.g. "man" in " "man"
is a noun", whereas the quotation, " "man" " in
this case, consists of the quoted expression *and* the
quotes.

The *rationale* of using quotes is, I think, widely mis-
understood by contemporary logicians. Instead of saying that quotes signalize a special use of the quoted
expression, many logicians use the terms "mention"
and "use" as though they were mutually exclusive—as
though a 'mentioned' (i.e. quoted) expression were not
at the same time being used. They would say that when
an expression is quoted, not it but the corresponding

---

[1] There is very little practical risk of confusing the two uses of
quotes, so readers may find this precaution rather like the White
Knight's armouring his horse's legs against possible sharkbites. But
once bitten, twice shy—I have actually been criticized in print for
lack of 'rigour' because I used scare-quotes in a logical article without
warning my readers that I was doing so.

quotation is being used; and that although the quotation is *physically* built up out of the quoted expression and a pair of encircling quotes, the quoted expression is not *logically* or *syntactically* a part of the quotation, any more than the word "man" is logically a part of the word "emancipate", or the variable "*x*" of the word "*six*". Some logicians, it seems, would even deny that the quotation " "man" " is logically a part of the quotation " "man is mortal" "; a quotation is held to be, logically speaking, a single long word, whose parts have no separate significance. (QUINE (2), p. 26.)

This last view is clearly wrong. A quoted series of expressions is always a series of quoted expressions; the quotes around a complex expression are to be read as applying to each syntactically distinct part of the expression; and if we fail so to read them, because we cannot discern the syntactical parts of the quoted expression, then we likewise fail to understand the quotation—we do not know what it is a quotation *of*. The quotation " "man is mortal" " does not indeed contain the quotation " "man" " as a physical part, i.e. it does not contain "man" *directly* enclosed in a pair of quotes; but it does logically or syntactically contain " "man" " as a part, for the single pair of quotes in " "man is mortal" " is to be read as applied to the three quoted words "man", "is", and "mortal" severally. If we use an ampersand "&" to mean "followed by", then "man" & "is" & "mortal" is just the expression "man is mortal"; I should maintain that the quotation " "man is mortal" " is rightly understood only if we read it as meaning the same as " "man" & "is" & "mortal" ", i.e. read it as *describing* the quoted expression in terms of the expressions it contains and

their order.[1] This result—that quotation of a complex
expression must be taken as *describing* the expression
in terms of its parts—is vital for our purpose; if in
"they said "let us destroy them together" " the
quotation were a single, logically unanalysable, word
and not a complex description, there would be a breakdown, at the very outset, of the idea that *oratio recta*
is a system of description applied in the first instance
to actual written or spoken language and secondarily
to thought.

In regard to the question whether a sign is to be
counted as occurring in a context in which it is quoted,
Quine argues as follows. Let us suppose that "Cicero"
occurs, in a logically relevant way, within " "Cicero"
has six letters", and "Tully" similarly within " "Tully"
has six letters". Then, Quine holds, the identity of
Tully with Cicero would allow us to interchange these
personal names, in the context of quotation marks as
in any other context (*salva veritate*, that is to say);
hence we could pass from the truth " "Cicero" has six
letters" to " "Tully" has six letters"; which is absurd.
(QUINE (2), p. 26.)

The crucial step of the above argument is contained
in the words (which are Quine's own): "the identity of
Tully with Cicero would allow us to interchange these
personal names, in the context of quotation marks as
in any other context". This is an application of a

---

[1] The difficulty in making this point is largely an accident of our
notation. We might well have decided to symbolize quotation by
underlining the syntactically simple parts of the quoted expression;
in that case, "man is mortal" would correspond both to " "man is
mortal" " and to " "man" & "is" & "mortal" ", and it would be as
easy to see that the quotation "man" is syntactically part of the
quotation "man is mortal" as that the quoted expression "man" or
man is part of the quoted expression "man is mortal" or man is
mortal.

logical law, which we may fittingly call "Leibniz's Law", that two names of the same thing are mutually replaceable *salva veritate*. But why is Quine so sure that Leibniz's Law admits of no exceptions? We cannot *both* hold this *and* treat 'occurrences' of expressions within quotes as genuine occurrences of them; but, so far as I can see, we might simply regard Quine's argument as proving that Leibniz's Law does not always hold. But further, Quine's own words, used to introduce Leibniz's Law into the argument, raise difficulties if his own view of quotations is accepted. What does he mean by "these personal names"? Plainly, the names "Tully" and "Cicero". But has he, on his own view, the right so to refer to them, when he has not mentioned them before (but only *used* them)? Let us waive this, and write out explicitly: "the identity of Tully with Cicero would allow us to interchange "Tully" and "Cicero" *salva veritate*"; or, still more clearly: "if Tully is identical with Cicero, then "Tully" and "Cicero" are interchangeable *salva veritate*". In order to accept this as (a case of) a sound principle of inference, we must recognize its logical form—we must be able to see that the same pair of names occur un-quoted in the antecedent and quoted in the consequent (as I should say), or are used in the antecedent and mentioned in the consequent (as the current jargon has it). But according to Quine the logician's eye can no more see "Tully" and "Cicero" in the consequent than it can see "man" in "emancipated"; so the way in which this application of Leibniz's Law is made is something that, on his own principles, Quine ought not to understand.

The indispensability of quotation is recognized in the practice of logicians, in the expository parts of their works; I can see no justification for their not attempting to construct formal systems with a device corresponding to quotation. (For a pioneer investigation, see REACH.) It would of course be out of place to attempt such a formal construction in this work.

Admittedly many 'quotations' are not logically part of the text at all, but serve rather as illustrations or diagrams. For example, in the discussion of the Existentialist in §4 I used quotes (as the reader may verify) to enclose bits of sheer nonsense. If quotation marks are always to be used as a logical sign, this will be incorrect; an added logical sign cannot turn sheer nonsense into sense, and so in a logically well-formed quotation the quoted expression must be a genuine bit of language. But it is quite easy to rewrite the discussion so as to make it no longer open to this objection, as follows:

Nothing noths	He judged that Nothing nothed
Figure 1.	Figure 2.

Suppose that an Existentialist utters in a tone of conviction sounds transcribable as in Figure 1, then I could not use Figure 2 as a report in written English of what he judged; for neither Figure 1 nor Figure 2 is a genuine bit of English. I ought rather to say: "He uttered sounds transcribable as in Figure 1, under the impression that they mean something that is true".

I think one source of the accepted contrast between 'use' and 'mention' is a wrong assimilation of quotations generally to the untypical quotations of §4. Properly speaking, these are not quotations at all; we cannot *quote* sheer nonsense, we can only parrot it, or copy its visible pattern, or make believe that it is (say) English and that we are reading it aloud. Here I am not including under "sheer nonsense" nonsensical combinations of genuine signs; for, as I have said, a complex quotation is to be read as a *description*, telling us that the quoted expression consists of such-and-such signs in such an order; and this description, if the signs are genuine, quotable, signs, is always significant, even if the signs in that order do not make up a well-formed expression.

There is an important logical point to be made about equiform expressions (i.e. expressions of the same sensible form) in different languages; let us say German "ja" (= "yes") and Polish "ja" (= "I"). I hold that the following syllogism involves a fallacy of equivocation:

"The word "ja" is a personal pronoun in Polish;
The word "ja" is a sign of affirmation in German;
Ergo, some word that is a personal pronoun in Polish is a sign of affirmation in German."

For the Polish word "ja", which is a personal pronoun, is simply a different word from the German word "ja", which is not; and it is hard to imagine circumstances in which one and the same bit of written or spoken language would be an instance of both words simultaneously. (One might imagine a man, who had been asked one question by a Pole in Polish and another question by a German in German, answering them both at once with a monosyllabic utterance that meant "I" to the Pole and "yes" to the German.) Quotation of a word is, on my view, use of the word; and a quotation of the Polish word "ja" will not also be quotation of the German word "ja", any more than any other use of the one word is also use of the other.

In the first premise of our 'syllogism' the quotation " "ja" " contains the Polish word, and in the second premise the equiform quotation " "ja" " contains the German word; the phrases "in Polish" and "in German" logically attach not to the predicates of these premises but to the subject—they serve to show which word is being quoted, the German or the Polish word. An understanding of this point will be needed in order to refute certain fallacious arguments in the next Section.

19

FALLACIOUS ARGUMENTS AGAINST PSYCHOLOGICAL USES OF *ORATIO RECTA*

THOUGH the primary use of *oratio recta* is to report a use of the quoted expression, it can be used, and is often used, instead of *oratio obliqua*, in order to report the use of words tantamount to those quoted. Can we then dispense with *oratio obliqua* and stick to *oratio recta*? For example: Is "James said that man is mortal" satisfactorily replaceable by "James said something tantamount to: "man is mortal" "? If not, then it would appear even more hopeless to try to report judgments by an analogical use of *oratio recta*. But, as my illustrations from the King James Bible show, judgments and thoughts *can* be reported this way; we know, then, in advance that any arguments against the satisfactoriness of *oratio recta* for the purpose must be fallacious.

One such argument is as follows. The statement

G

"James said something tantamount to: "man is mortal" " is unsatisfactory as it stands; for the quoted expression might be an expression of some language other than English, and might in that language not mean that man is mortal. But if we insert "the English expression" after "tantamount to", then the resulting statement will not do as a substitution for "James said that man is mortal"; for *this* statement makes no reference to the English language, though it is made in English. (*Cf.* CHURCH.)

To this I reply that against the possible ambiguity here alleged no provision is practically necessary, and none is theoretically sufficient. Theoretically, the framework in which the quotation " "man is mortal" " occurs might likewise be equiform with an expression of some exotic language; and no provisos, sub-intents, and saving clauses inserted in the framework can remove this theoretical risk, for the exotic language might contain expressions equiform to them also. In practice, if I say to a normal English-speaking adult "James said something tantamount to "man is mortal" " he will both understand the framework of the quotation, as an English expression, and understand what expression I am intending to quote; there is no practical risk of misunderstanding if I fail to insert "the English expression" after "tantamount to".

The argument just considered gets its plausibility from an assumption that *one and the same* expression "man is mortal" could occur both in English and in some exotic language, with different meanings; in that case, we could not mean anything definite by "tantamount to: "man is mortal" " if we failed to specify the language in which "man is mortal" is to be taken to be. But, as I argued just now, an expression in an exotic language, equiform to the English expression "man is mortal" but different in meaning, would just be *a different expression*. Explicit mention of English would be needed only if one's hearer were likely not to know that the quotation " "man is mortal" " is a quotation of the English expression; in practice it is not necessary.

Another argument against replacing *oratio obliqua* by *oratio recta* is this. If a sentence containing a quotation is translated, the quoted expression must be left untranslated; for the translation must be a statement about the same expression as the original sentence was about, and therefore must contain quotation of that expression, not of some other. But if a sentence contains *oratio obliqua*, then this must be translated; e.g. the clause "man is mortal" in *oratio obliqua* would become in Latin "*hominem esse mortalem*". So, since "James said something tantamount to "man is mortal" " is essentially different, in its behaviour under translation, from "James said that man is mortal", it cannot be a satisfactory *Ersatz* for it. (Once more, *cf.* CHURCH.)

It is true that if we construct an *oratio-recta Ersatz* for "James said that man is mortal" we shall use the quotation " "man is mortal" ", whereas if we construct such an *Ersatz* in Latin for "*Jacobus dixit hominem esse mortalem*" we shall have to use the quotation " "*homo est mortalis*" "; and it may seem obvious that the one quotation is not a translation of the other. But the one quotation will occur in the context "tantamount to: "man is mortal" "; the other will occur in a Latin context translatable as: "tantamount to: "*homo est mortalis*" ". Now these contexts *are* equivalent; for "tantamount to: "*homo est mortalis*" ", the English version of the Latin context, is substitutable in many English sentences, *salva veritate*, for "tantamount to: "man is mortal" ", since an expression is tantamount to "*homo est mortalis*" if and only if it is tantamount to "man is mortal". Moreover, only a person who knows both English and Latin will understand "tantamount to "*homo est mortalis*" ", since otherwise he would not know what expression was being quoted; but for such a person the description "tantamount to: "*homo est mortalis*" " is of the same force as "tantamount to: "man is mortal" ". It follows that the Latin context of which "tantamount to: "*homo est mortalis*" " is a translation is likewise of the same force as "tantamount to "man is mortal" ". Thus, although in general an English sentence containing the quotation " "man is mortal" " is not fairly rendered by a Latin sentence correspondingly containing the quotation " "*homo est mortalis*" "; nevertheless the Latin *oratio-recta Ersatz* for "*Jacobus dixit hominem esse mortalem*", which would use the latter quotation, *is* a reasonable equivalent of the English *Ersatz* for "James said that man is mortal", which would use the former quotation.

Somebody may complain that it is not enough for the English *Ersatz* and the Latin *Ersatz* to be 'reasonably equivalent' to one another, since the sentences they replace are *synonymous*; if they are only 'reasonably equivalent', something important has been lost. I should demand of such a critic: "What is your criterion of synonymy?"—with very little hope of getting a coherent answer. (On the obscurity of the term "synonymous", see QUINE (3).) Two expressions are equivalent to the extent to which they are intersubstitutable *salva veritate*; but we cannot define synonymy as a supreme degree of equivalence, intersubstitutability *salva veritate* in *all* contexts; for if occurrence in quotation is recognized, *no* two distinct (non-equiform) expressions are intersubstitutable *salva veritate* at *all* occurrences. E.g. there is a high degree of equivalence between "furze" and "gorse", but "furze" is not substitutable for "gorse" *salva veritate* in " "gorse" rhymes with "horse" ". Nor could we say that synonymy is intersubstitutability of expressions *salva veritate* at all non-quoted occurrences. For then, in order to know whether "furze" and "gorse" are synonymous, we should have to know whether "furze" can be substituted *salva veritate* for the first occurrence of "gorse" in "Any statement made about gorse is tantamount to the same statement made about gorse"; i.e. whether any statement made about furze is tantamount to the same statement made about gorse; and to know this we should have to know *already* whether "furze" and "gorse" are synonyms. So no objection stated in terms of "synonymy" is going to have much weight; an attempt to define "synonymy" strictly is likely either to yield a relation that never holds between non-equiform expressions, or to involve a vicious circle when we try to apply it. For this reason I have deliberately used familiar words like "equivalent" and "tantamount to" rather than "synonymous"; there is less danger that way of making a show of precision where precision is not attainable. (Carnap's talk of "intensional isomorphism" is even worse; for the term is just as vague as "synonymy", but is even more calculated to give the impression that scientific rigour has been achieved.)

"Correct translation" is of course just as imprecise a term as "synonymy". Very often, what we count as a correct translation will include translation of quoted expressions; a translator of *Quo Vadis* would not feel obliged to leave all the conversations in the original Polish, and we should count it as perversely wrong, not pedantically correct, if he did so. Translating on this principle, we should get in the Latin version of "James said something tantamount to "man is mortal" " the quotation " "*homo est mortalis*" " rather than " "man is mortal" ": reasonably so, because nothing is being asserted of "man is mortal" that is not equally true of "*homo est mortalis*". But then the 'translation' argument against the *oratio-recta Ersatz* of "James said that man is a rational animal" breaks down.

What about double *oratio obliqua*? The *Ersatz* for "Smith says that James says that man is mortal" would be: "Smith says something tantamount to: "James says something tantamount to: "Man is mortal" " ". What I have already said about 'reasonable' equivalence, replaceability *salva veritate*, and correct translation all carries over to this more complex case; I shall not here work the matter out in detail, but I do not think any new problem arises.

20

QUANTIFICATION INTO *ORATIO OBLIQUA* AND *ORATIO RECTA*

A PROBLEM we must certainly tackle is that of *quantifying into* (to use Quine's expression) *oratio obliqua* and *oratio recta*. So simple a psychological statement as "More people came than he thought would come" involves 'quantifying into' *oratio obliqua*; one might try to show its quantification as follows:

(A) "For some number n, more than n people came, and he thought that at most n people would come",

where the quantifier "for some number n" is meant to be picked up by (to 'bind') an occurrence of "n" in an *oratio obliqua* clause. But such a simple analysis will not do; in fact, there are plausible arguments to show that it is always nonsense to 'quantify into' *oratio obliqua* (see QUINE (3), chap. viii).—One of the difficulties is to assign a *range* to a quantification "for some x" that reaches into *oratio obliqua*; to answer the question "some *what*?"—Quine's argument is certainly too sweeping in its conclusion, because it is certainly quite intelligible to say "More people came than he thought would come". We must try, then, to get round the conclusion. If we can do this by our method of using *oratio recta* as *Ersatz* for *oratio obliqua*, this will be a point in favour of the method.

Let us begin with quantification into plain *oratio recta*. Suppose a letter I get from Smith contains the words: "James says one of his colleagues "is out on bail after arrest on a serious charge"; I am not at liberty to give you his name". I assume Smith's meaning to be that James used the actual words "is out on bail after arrest on a serious charge". A first shot at making explicit the quantification in Smith's statement might run like this:

(A) "For some x, x is one of James's colleagues and James says "x is out on bail after arrest on a serious charge" ".

There are, however, two troubles about (A). First, if we interpret the quotation within (A) in the ordinary way, then the variable "x" would have to be the actual expression used by James to refer to his unlucky colleague—which is improbable. Secondly, though it is all right to use a proper name first unquoted and then quoted, as in:

(B) "Johnson is one of James's colleagues, and James says "Johnson is out on bail after arrest on a serious charge" ",

there are both technical difficulties and difficulties of interpretation about replacing the two occurrences of "Johnson" by occurrences of the variable "x", both bound by the same quantifier. We need not here discuss technical difficulties; what makes such a use of "x" hard to interpret at all is that we cannot consistently interpret "For some x, . . . x . . ." in (A) as meaning "There is some person who . . .", nor yet as meaning "There is some word which . . ." The first interpretation is ruled out by the quoted occurrence of "x"; for, even if we waive the objection that this ought to refer to an actual use of "x" by James, it certainly ought to refer to something that James said; and a person cannot be part of what somebody else said. The second interpretation is equally ruled out by the unquoted occurrences of "x"; a word cannot be somebody's colleague. But there is an easy way out of our troubles. If we use the ampersand, as in §17, for 'concatenation' (i.e. to mean "followed by"), we may express what Smith presumably meant as follows:

(C) "For some x, one of James's colleagues has the name x, and what James said was x & "is out on bail after arrest on a serious charge" ".

Consider now a quantification into *oratio obliqua*: "More people came to Smith's party than James said would come". A first shot at analysing this would be:

(D) "For some *n*, more than *n* people came to Smith's party, and James said that at most *n* people would come to Smith's party".

As before, there are difficulties over the interpretation of the variable; but they can be got over fairly easily if we resort to an *oratio recta* paraphrase:

(E) "For some *numeral n*, "more than" & *n* & "people came to Smith's party" is a true statement, and James said something to this effect: "at most" & *n* & "people will come to Smith's party" ".

(E) is obtainable by existential quantification from a statement like:

(F) " "More than twenty people came to Smith's party" is a true statement, and James said something to this effect: "at most twenty people will come to Smith's party" ".

For, using our ampersand, we may rewrite (F) thus:

(F') " "More than" & "twenty" & "people came to Smith's party" is a true statement, and James said something to this effect: "at most" & "twenty" & "people will come to Smith's party" ".

(E) appears reasonably close to the way one would intend "more people came to Smith's party than James said would come"; the quantification in (E) will be seen to relate to *expressions*, not to the 'intensional entities' sometimes brought into such analyses. If now we want instead an analysis of "more people came to Smith's party than James *thought* would come", all we have to do is to replace "James said" in (E) by "James said in his heart".

21

THE PREDICATE "TRUE"

THE ROLE of the predicate "is a true statement" in (E) of §20 should be noticed. In (F) of §20 the use of "is true" or "is a true statement" is superfluous; we could cancel out these words along with the pair of opening and closing quotes preceding them:

(F″) "More than twenty people came to Smith's party, and James said something to the effect: "at most twenty people will come to Smith's party" ".

The expression "is (a) true (statement)" is like the sign " ♮ " in musical notation. After the sign " ♯ ", all notes written on the "C" line of the stave are to be read as meaning C sharp; but the sign " ♮ " cancels the preceding " ♯ ", and thereafter such notes are to be read as meaning C natural. Similarly, we write a statement in quotes in order to *mention* that statement; if we now write after it "is (a) true (statement)", this cancels the quotes, and it is as though we simply *used* the quoted statement. By the current false doctrine about 'use and mention' this simple point has been made quite unintelligible; since the logician is supposed to turn a blind eye to the occurrences of expressions within quotes (each quotation being regarded as one long word, logically unanalysable), he must make believe that he does not see the rationale of the inference (say) from "man is mortal" to " "man is mortal" is true" and conversely. The genuine significance of "true" is thus missed, and then queer 'theories' and 'definitions' of truth are framed.

If "is true" thus cancels out with the preceding pair

of quotes, why not simply write down the statement that is being presented as true, without quotes and without any use of "true"? Is not the word "true" superfluous? No, for we cannot *always* do this cancelling-out; we cannot do it with "What the policeman said was true", nor can we do it in (E) of §20. Again, "if "every man" is a true statement" is a perfectly intelligible protasis to a hypothetical statement, but "if every man" is not; here again the cancelling-out is unworkable. It is only when a genuine statement is being quoted in full that we can use "is (a) true (statement)" to cancel the enclosing quotes.

We must not think that the role of "the statement ". . . " is true" is that of a (Fregean) assertion sign; and again, "What the policeman said is true" does not mean something like "I corroborate what the policeman said". For "is true" can stand quite happily in an "if" clause, which is not asserted; to say "if the statement "the Earth is flat" is true, astronomy is bunkum" does not commit the speaker to asserting that the Earth is flat. Again, "if what the policeman said is true" is not at all the same thing as "if I corroborate what the policeman said". In main clauses, to be sure, "I corroborate" has a 'performatory' role—its utterance is an act of corroborating—and it loses this role in an "if" clause; but this very fact shows how differently "I corroborate" works from "is true", which can go into an "if" clause without any change of its ordinary role.

When I say " "jam dies" is true in Latin if it is now day", "in Latin" logically attaches not to "is true" but to the quotation " "jam dies" "; we cannot argue that because "jam dies" is false in English, there is something true in Latin but false in English—this is a crude equivocation, already exposed. The English "jam dies" and the Latin "jam dies" are simply different expressions; the former is used (quoted) in " "jam dies" is false in English", and the latter in " "jam dies" is true in Latin when it is now day"; you may convince yourself of this by reading the two sentences aloud. The 'semantic' theory that "in Latin" and "in English" could qualify the predicate "true" is thus a howler; whatever paradoxes like the Liar may arise, no solution in terms of "true-in-L" and "true-in-M" is acceptable.

I have been trying to make out that "true" is a predicate properly and primarily applicable to statements in language, rather than to thoughts or judgments or objective 'intensional entities'. This contention is a necessary part of my general thesis—that language about thoughts is an analogical development of language about language.

22

COMBINATION OF OUR TWO THEORIES OF JUDGMENT

HOW IS THIS account of judgment related to the account given in §14? That first account was both sketchy and schematic: sketchy, in that I discussed only a few sample judgments; schematic, in that I used two uninterpreted terms—"Idea" and "§". The latter expression was used quite formalistically; "§" was an unspecified logical operator upon relative terms. "Idea" on the other hand was not wholly uninterpreted; Smith's Idea *every man* would be an exercise of his concept *every man*, which in turn, on my explanation, is a mental capacity exercised in judgments that are expressible by use of the words "every man". But "Idea" could still be very variously interpreted, conformably to these rough explanations. Now can interpretations of "Idea" and of "§" be found within the limits of our *oratio recta* system for describing judgments?

Let us provisionally say that Smith's Idea *every man* consists in his saying-in-his-heart something to the same effect as "every man" (which, let me repeat, need not consist in his having mental images of these or other words). I shall say "mental utterance of" as an abbreviation for "saying-in-his-heart something to the same effect as"; thus, Smith's Idea *every man* is Smith's mental utterance of "every man"; and "Smith's Idea of [an Idea of *every man*]" will be interpreted as "Smith's mental utterance of "a mental utterance of "every man" " ". This satisfies the condition, stated on p. 57, that once we understand "Idea" and the construction of " every man " in " Idea of *every man* " we must already have all the logical devices we need in order to understand "Smith's Idea of [an Idea of *every man*]". For "Smith's mental utterance of "a mental utterance of "every man" " " is understandable so long as we understand "mental utterance" and also understand the logic of quotations.

In order that the relation §(sharper than) should hold between two Ideas, there must be a judgment that . . . is sharper than ——; that is, in our present language, a mental utterance of some statement using "(is) sharper than". (Let us, to simplify matters, erase the word "blunter" from the language we are using to describe judgments, and replace it by "conversely sharper".) What we need is some relation %(sharper than), definable in terms of "sharper than", satisfying this condition: When Smith's judgment consists of an Idea α in the relation §(sharper than) to an Idea β, then there are expressions A, B, C, such that α, β are Smith's mental utterances of A, B, respectively, and Smith's judgment as a whole is a mental utterance of C, and any (physical) occurrence of C consists of an occurrence of A in the relation %(sharper than) to an occurrence of B. If we could actually define " %(sharper than)", we should have completed the interpretation of our former theory of judgments in terms of our *oratio recta* system for describing them.

Now we can at least see the main outlines of the definition of " %(sharper than)". Let us define "†(sharper than)" as follows; x is in the relation †(sharper than) to y if and only if: x and y are utterances of the same person, and there are expressions X and Y such that x is the utterance of X, and y of Y, in that person's utterance *either* of X & "is" & "sharper than" & Y *or* of Y & "is conversely" & "sharper than" & X. (The ampersand is as before the sign of 'concatenation'.) For example, if the person had said out loud "some knife is sharper than some spoon", or if he had said "some spoon is conversely sharper than some knife", in either case his utterance of "some knife" would have been in the relation †(sharper than) to his utterance of "some spoon"; if, on the other hand, he had said "some spoon is sharper than some knife", then his utterance of "some spoon" would have been in the relation †(sharper than) to his utterance of "some knife". It is because we make relations like †(sharper than) hold between utterances of expressions, that we are able to talk about the relation *sharper than* effectively—just having the relative term "sharper than" would not suffice unless we used it to establish the relation †(sharper than) between expressions. (This point is

made, rather obscurely, in Wittgenstein's *Tractatus*.)
It is no objection to our using such a relation in explaining the relation §(sharper than), that in the *definiens* of
"†(sharper than)" there is a non-extensional (quoted)
occurrence of "sharper than"; for I said already in §13
that the operator "§" must be regarded as non-extensional.[1]

We cannot regard the relation %(sharper than) as
actually being the relation †(sharper than); for it is
easily seen that Smith's utterance of "some knife"
would stand in the relation †(sharper than) to his
utterance of "any spoon" alike in the utterance "some
knife is sharper than any spoon" and in the utterance
"any spoon is conversely sharper than some knife";
whereas the corresponding judgments are different.
But this only means that the definition of " %(sharper
than) would have to be more complicated than the
above definition of "†(sharper than)".

23

DANGERS OF THE 'INNER LANGUAGE' ANALOGY

THE IMPORTANT thing about analogical extensions of a concept is that we should know (in practice at any rate) how far to carry the analogy. Some
people have certainly carried the analogy of thought to

---

[1] In an 'extensional' logic the Leibniz law of §18 would hold unrestrictedly, and predicates or relative terms would be freely intersubstitutable provided that they held good of the same objects (*cf.* §14). Our language, since it contains *quoted* occurrences of expressions, is easily shown not to be 'extensional' in either respect.

language too far. Thus, for William of Ockham, besides
the spoken, conventional, languages, all men have a
common, natural, language; for convenience, I shall
call it "Mental". The grammar of Mental turns out to
be remarkably like Latin grammar. There are nouns
and verbs in Mental; nouns have cases and numbers,
and verbs have voice, mood, tense, number, and person.
On the other hand, there is nothing in Mental corresponding to the different Latin declensions and conjugations; nor are there any deponent verbs in Mental.
Ockham's criterion for transferring Latin grammatical
terms to Mental was very simple-minded. Nouns of
different declensions, or verbs of different conjugations,
may be synonyms, and then presumably correspond to
the same Mental noun or verb; so there is no reason
to ascribe differences of declension or conjugation to
Mental words. But a change of case or number or voice
may quite alter the sense of a Latin sentence; so Mental
words must have case, number, and voice.

Without being able to say just how far the analogy
of inner language can be carried, I think men of good
sense would see immediately that Ockham carries it
much too far. He merely transfers features of Latin
grammar to Mental, and then regards this as explaining
why such features occur in Latin—they are needed there
if what we say inwardly in Mental is to be outwardly
got across to others in Latin. But clearly nothing
is explained at all. Presumably Ockham's reasons for
thinking that the supposed grammar of Mental had
explanatory force were that Mental is a natural and
universal language, and that Mental words, unlike
Latin words, are immaterial entities. But if all men had
a natural and universal *spoken* language, that would
not mean that its grammar was any more self-explana-

tory than Latin grammar. And what carries significance in a language is its structure, not its medium—
the structure that can be transferred from spoken to
written language and to Morse code; but Ockham takes
for granted the grammatical structure of Latin, and
supposes that Mental, unlike Latin, is intrinsically
intelligible, simply because its medium is not material
but spiritual. In point of fact, any problems that arise
as to the significance of a grammatical device will arise
equally for the alleged Mental uses of this device; and
Ockham's saying that the words of Mental are immaterial would merely raise such footling problems as how
something immaterial can be in the genitive case, without throwing any light on the use of the genitive. To
do Ockham justice, he wastes little time on such futili-
ties; most of his, often acute, enquiries into the logical
syntax of Latin are undisturbed by the reflection that
Latin is really an imperfect reproduction of the Mental
original, which on his view is the proper study of a
logician.

A little consideration will show us various points at
which the analogy of inner language must break down.
The grammatical properties ascribed by Ockham to
Mental words may all be easily dismissed, except mood
and tense. "The farmer has one donkey, which is white"
and "the farmer's one donkey is white" plainly both
express the same judgment, although the cases of
"farmer" and "donkey" are different in the two sentences; and so for most of the grammatical attributes.
Tense, however, does enter into the content of our
thoughts; "the farmer has often been drunk" cannot
be replaced by any sentence to the same effect in which
the tense is future instead of past. And I am inclined to
think that there are also modal differences between

H

thoughts—though the moods of a natural language like
Latin are a very inadequate indication of this, being
cluttered with a lot of logically insignificant idiomatic
uses.

What is more important is the difference between
speech and thought as regards temporal duration.
Spoken words last so long in physical time, and one
word comes out after another; the time they take is, as
Aquinas would say, the sort of time that is the measure
of local motion—one could sensibly say that the utterance of the words was simultaneous with the movement
of a body, e.g. the hand of a clock, from one place
to another. The same would go for the duration of
mental images of words, or any other mental images;
one could sensibly say "I rehearsed the words in my
head as I watched the beetle crawl from one side of the
table to the other".

With a thought it is quite different. Even if we
accepted the view sketched in §14 that a judgment is a
complex of Ideas, we could hardly suppose that in a
thought the Ideas occur successively, as the words do
in a sentence; it seems reasonable to say that unless the
whole complex content is grasped all together—unless
the Ideas, if Ideas there are, are all simultaneously
present—the thought or judgment just does not exist
at all. All the same, when we read of the French poli-
tician who maintained that in French the word-order
perfectly represented the order in thought (WITTGEN-
STEIN, Part I, §336), our first reaction may be e.g. to
think of the French negative "ne . . . pas", and protest
that even a Frenchman could not negate the 'verb'
part of his judgment in two bits, half an act of negation preceding the 'verb' part and half an act following
it; that is to say, we are inclined to think that the Ideas

do have *a* temporal order, only not quite the same order as that of the French words expressing them. Only on further reflection do we come to the view that there can be no question of their occurring in *any* temporal order. On my analysis of judgment in terms of Ideas that which corresponded to the 'main verb' in the verbal expression of judgment would be, not an Idea, but the relation binding the Ideas together; and it would be plainly absurd to enquire which position of the main verb best corresponded to the temporal position of this relation as compared with the Ideas it relates. Of course that analysis was only tentative and provisional; at the same time, it was suggested to me by the rather stringent requirements of logic, which became apparent in criticizing Russell's theory; it seems most unlikely that analysis of a judgment as a temporal succession of Ideas could meet these requirements, whatever temporal order we assume.

If a judgment is a non-successive unity, it seems to follow that we cannot assign to judgment more than a loose connexion with physical time. First, could a judgment be regarded as occupying a mere moment of physical time? If so, then either in any finite stretch of time there would be an illimitable number of judgments (or other thoughts), or there would be flashes of thought at discrete instants separated by gaps of thoughtlessness; the first alternative at least is plainly false, but the second might seem possible. Let us consider, however, the time-relation between an act of judgment and the words that express it. Once the words have been spoken, we suppose, the man goes on to think of other matters; so the act cannot be put later than the utterance of the end of the last word. If the man was not in a position to rehearse his words mentally before he said them, the act of judgment might be said not to come before the beginning of the utterance. Let us further suppose that the man's attention is not distracted while he speaks. Are we now to say that the judgment occurs in just one instant of the utterance, the rest of the time being taken up with uttering parrotwise? or, that it is repeated in a series of flashes, so as to keep the utterance on the right track?

Or are we rather to say that the judging is going on continuously during the utterance? That is worse nonsense than ever: one can say "at 12.10 I had a sudden stab of pain, and the pain went on for two minutes", but not: "at 12.10 I had a sudden thought, and the thought lasted just long enough for me to utter it—it went on all the while that I was uttering it, and then it stopped". All that we can say is that the judgment is loosely bound up with physical time, in that (e.g.) it did not occur before the beginning or after the end of the words in which it is uttered; if we try to assign it to a definite moment or moments, or to a definite stretch of time, we find ourselves in a bog of nonsense.

What I have just said about the 'loose' relation of judgments to physical time is a logical point about applying time-specifications in our discourse about judgments; it does not imply e.g. that judgments are really performed in a super-physical realm. Excluding certain questions about the time of judgments as unreasonable can have no such momentous consequences; and for judgments to be tied loosely to physical time is still for them to be tied.

24

THE NOTION OF 'INNER SENSE'

IN INVESTIGATING some other psychological concepts, I shall approach them from the side of psychological judgments in which they are exercised. Psychological judgments have very often been held to be based primarily on the deliverances of an 'inner sense' whereby we are cognizant every one of his own psychical states; just as judgments about physical realities are based on the evidence of our senses. The supposed 'inner sense' is compared sometimes to looking ('introspection'), sometimes to feeling.

With the ordinary senses there is associated the power of forming mental images; I see in my mind's eye past scenes that are no longer before me, or things that I might see now in another position, or even quite imaginary scenes. No mental images, however, are commonly assigned to 'inner sense' in the same way. People have ridiculed the idea of McTaggart that I may have mental images of my own past mental states which I have introspectively perceived, of other people's mental states which I happen to be unable to inspect (a removable limitation, McTaggart believed), and of purely imaginary mental states that nobody has actually been in. (MCTAGGART, pp. 106–8.) Of course McTaggart's idea is quite wrong, but why is it absurd? If "looking into the mind" has a genuine logical similarity to "looking into the box", then it ought to make sense to talk about introspective mental images as we do about visual images; lack of introspective imagery would be an idiosyncrasy like being unable to visualize, and might be expected to disable a man for some tasks. If McTaggart's idea is absurd, then it ought to make us suspect the comparison of introspection to real looking.

Hume seems to have supposed that there were mental images of past mental states—less vivid copies of them, related to them as a perfume I 'smell' in memory is to something I really smell. But what Hume says is shot all through with his confusion between two senses of "idea"—the mental image of something, and the exercise of a concept of it in judgment. This exercise is in no way dependent on the presence of a pale replica of the thing judged about; if it were, then, as St Augustine remarked, we should habitually feel a certain reluctance to use the words "grief", "fear", "pain", lest they should arouse in our minds faint reproductions of the unwelcome experiences so called (*Confessions*, book X, chap. xiv).[1]

People suppose that I can give meaning to such words as "seeing", "hearing", "thinking", "hoping", etc., only by observing in my own case sample occurrences of what these words refer to; failing the relevant experiences, or failing attention to them when I have had them, I must either lack a concept altogether or possess it in a very imperfect form, comparable to a colour-blind man's concept of colours. Let us fasten upon this comparison. The defect colour-blindness can be tested for, not only by looking for oddities in a man's colour-concepts, which show in his use of colour-words, but also by a non-linguistic investigation of what colours he is practically able to discriminate,

[1] Augustine here uses the term "*notiones*" for the mental acts involved in an understanding of such words as "fear", and denies that *notiones* are *imagines*. I wonder if this is the origin of Berkeley's puzzling talk about 'notions' as opposed to 'ideas'.

without using words. We can even investigate what colour-discriminations brutes are capable of, although of course they cannot tell us and have no colour-concepts at all. Now could there be, let us say, anger-fear emotion-blindness, as there can be red-green colour-blindness? Could a man's introspective 'sense' be unable to discriminate between his being angry and his being afraid, so that his use of the words "anger" and "fear" depended precariously on other people's use of them, in the way that a colour-blind man's use of colour-words does? In regard to colours, we can distinguish between a colour-blind man with a sensory defect and a mentally defective man who is unable to form colour-concepts and learn the use of colour-words; could we make a similar distinction about emotions? Could we say of somebody: "He's very intelligent, but he keeps on using words for emotions wrongly; the psychiatrist says he has a congenital defect of the 'inner sense' that discriminates emotions from each other"?

I chose to set emotion-words and colour-words side by side, because there really is a considerable logical similarity. Both colours and emotions can occur in different intensities, and can wax and wane in intensity; there can be an emotion that is a blend of anger and fear, as there is a colour that is a blend of red and blue; you can ask of a feeling of fear, as you can of a coloured light, whether it came on suddenly or gradually, and how long it lasted, etc. If in spite of this we find a radical dissimilarity between colour-language and emotion-language, in that we could not apply a term "emotion-blindness" comparably to "colour-blindness", then the conclusion we ought to draw is surely that the idea of an introspective 'sense' is an illusion.

Somebody might try saying that the reason why we have no use for the term "emotion-blindness" is that our 'inner sense' is not liable to such defects as our eyesight is; our inner sense represents our emotions just as they occur, even if we are unable to describe them correctly. Now a sense that was *in fact* not affected by any illusions, any failure to discriminate, etc., is indeed conceivable; but plainly what our present objection is really after is a sense that not merely does not but *cannot* mislead us. But this "cannot" would be a logical "cannot"; and the inclination to use "cannot" here points to a logical difference between our knowledge of the outer world by our senses and our knowledge of the mind by 'inner sense'. Of *bona fide* sense-faculties, it is impossible to say that they *cannot* be defective or inaccurate.

If anyone should think that in criticizing the idea of 'inner sense' I am flogging a dead horse, or knocking down a stuffed dummy of my own creation, I may reply by instancing Freud's use of the idea. "What role is there now left, in our representation of things, to the phenomena of consciousness, once so all-powerful and overshadowing all else? None other than *that of a sense-organ for the perception of psychic qualities*." (FREUD, p. 544; his italics.) "The unconscious is the true psychic reality; *in its inner nature it is just as much unknown to us as the reality of the external world, and it is just as imperfectly communicated to us by the data of consciousness as is the external world by the reports of our sense-organs*." (FREUD, p. 542; his italics.) Freud, as may be seen, transfers a naive 'representative' theory of perception from its usual application (to the bodily senses, that is), and holds it to be no less valid of 'inner sense'. Presumably on his view 'inner sense' would *not* be inerrant; but I find in him no clear account of what an error of 'inner sense' would be like.

25

COULD SENSUOUS EXPERIENCES OCCUR APART FROM AN ORGANISM?

'INNER SENSE' is supposed to show us, and to be the only thing that shows us, what it is like to see, hear, be afraid, etc. With this there goes a view that the connexion between such 'sensuous' experiences and a bodily organism is only a well-established empirical generalization. Such experiences are indeed dependent upon material things in the sense of being occupied with them; but they are not identifiable with any describable physiological processes in a living organism, and their connexion with such processes is only something empirically determined. There is no necessary, conceptual, connexion between the experience we call "seeing" and the processes that physiologists tell us happen in eye and brain; the statement "James can still see, although his optic centres are destroyed" is very unlikely on inductive grounds but perfectly intelligible—after all, people used the word "see" long before they had any idea of things happening in the optic centres of the brain. It therefore appears to be clearly conceivable that seeing and other 'sensuous' experiences might go on continuously even after the death of the organism with which they are now associated, and that the inductive reasons for doubting whether this ever happens might be outweighed by the evidence of Psychical Research.

I think it is an important conceptual enquiry to consider whether *really* disembodied seeing, hearing, pain, hunger, emotion, etc., are so clearly intelligible as is supposed in this common philosophical point of view. (I stress "really disembodied". Some people believe that there is a subtle body endowed with its own sense-organs, which persists after the dissolution of the body commonly so called. This view, so far as I can see, is philosophically speaking both unobjectionable and uninteresting. It is clear off-hand that the 'mind-body problem' is just the same whether the body is gross or subtle.)

"The verb 'to see' has its meaning for me because I *do* see—I have that experience!" Nonsense. As well suppose that I can come to know what a minus quantity is by setting out to lose weight. What shows a man to have the concept *seeing* is not merely that he sees, but that he can take an intelligent part in our everyday use of the word "seeing". Our concept of sight has its life only in connexion with a whole set of other concepts, some of them relating to the physical characteristics of visible objects, others relating to the behaviour of people who see things. (I express exercise of this concept in such utterances as "I can't see, it's too far off—now it's coming into view!" "He couldn't see me, he didn't look round", "I caught his eye", etc., etc.) It would be merely silly to be frightened off admitting this by the bogy of behaviourism; you can very well admit it without also thinking that "seeing" stands for a kind of behaviour.

Our investigation is put on the wrong track by an abstractionist prejudice. For an abstractionist, the possession of the concept *seeing* must be taken to be a capacity for finding and recognizing some recurrent feature—or at least to be that primarily; and I can find instances of seeing only in my own mind, by 'inner sense'; in other people I find nothing but characteristic pieces of behaviour, from which however it could justifiably be inferred (how?) that they also see.—In fact, of course, I learn to use the word "see" of others and of myself simultaneously; and if we reject the doctrine of abstractionism, we need not distinguish between exercises of the concept *seeing* as primary ones, when I catch myself in the act of seeing something, and secondary ones, when I (with great rashness, surely, on this view) form the judgment that others likewise see. To have the concept *seeing* is not even primarily a matter of being able to spot instances of a characteristic repeatedly given in my ('inner-sense') experiences; *no* concept is primarily a recognitional capacity. And the exercise of one concept is intertwined with the exercise of others; as with a spider's web, some connexions may be broken with impunity, but if you break enough the whole web collapses—the concept becomes unusable. Just such a collapse happens, I believe, when we try to think of seeing, hearing, pain, emotion, etc., going on independently of a body.

When I apply this sort of concept to a human being, I do so in connexion with a whole lot of other concepts that I apply to human beings and their natural environment. It is easy enough to extend the concepts of 'sensuous' experience to creatures fairly like human beings, such as cats, dogs, and horses; when we try to extend them to creatures extremely unlike human beings in their style of life, we feel, if we are wise, great uncertainty—not just uncertainty as to the facts, or as to the possibility of finding them out, but uncertainty as to the *meaning* of saying: "I now know how to tell when an earthworm is angry". One is of course tempted to say: "That's easy; an earthworm is angry if it is feeling the way I feel when I am angry!" But this is just like saying: "Of course I know what it is for the time on the Sun to be five o'clock; it is five o'clock on the Sun when it is the same time as when it is five o'clock here!" (WITTGENSTEIN, Part I, §350)—which clearly gets us no for'arder. There is just the same difficulty in extending the concept *the same time* as in extending the concept *five o'clock*. So in the psychological case: I know how to apply the concept *anger* to myself and to James, and I know how to apply the concept *feeling the same way* as between myself and James, or James and Smith; I get into the same difficulties if I try applying the concept *feeling the same way* as between myself and an earthworm as I do over applying the concept *anger* to it.[1]

Even an earthworm, though, affords some handholds for the application of 'sensuous' psychological concepts; we connect its writhings when injured with our own pain-reactions. But when it comes to an auto-

---

[1] On a point of interpretation, I think it is a mistake to read Wittgenstein as having intended to show that I cannot apply a concept like *anger* both to myself and to others, and that it is meaningless to speak of others' feeling the same way as I do (unless indeed I just mean that they behave as I do). The difficulty of transferring the concept *anger* from myself to others is a spurious one, arising from the abstractionism that Wittgenstein consistently rejected; and the solution that the term "anger" is an equivocal term, applied in my own case to a recurrent experience and in other cases to a recurrent pattern of behaviour, is plausible, I think, only on abstractionist presuppositions; I do not believe, as some people I have had discussion with apparently do, that Wittgenstein really held this view and only shrank from a brash statement of it.

maton, or again if we are invited to apply the concepts to a supposed disembodied existence, then we may be sure that we are right in refusing to play; too many threads are broken, and the conceptual web has collapsed. An automaton, by all sorts of criteria, is not even alive; we know this, though we may be uncertain whether to call a virus (say) alive or not. (Doctors may not agree whether a patient is yet dead; but we know that Queen Anne is dead.) Between what is certainly inanimate and ourselves there is far too little similarity for us to be able to pick out anything in its behaviour corresponding to the context in which we judge that human beings are in pain, or hungry, or afraid; we know that any particular movement which might even remotely suggest similarity is performed because the designer of the automaton intended such an imitation, and we ought to be no more inclined to ascribe feelings to the automaton than, after childhood, we think that a doll is in pain because it has been so constructed as to cry when it is smacked.—As for disembodied sensations and feelings, even more connexions are broken in this case; there is no handhold for applying 'sensuous' concepts to disembodied existence at all—we just do not know what we are doing if we try.

A good illustration, I think, of a concept's losing its applicability through connexions being broken is the following. Certain hysterics claimed to have magnetic sensations; it was discovered, however, that their claim to be having them at a given time did not go with the presence of a magnet in their neighbourhood but with their belief, true or false, that a magnet was there. It would now have been possible to say: "We must take the patients' word for it that they have these peculiar sensations, which are quite different from ordinary people's sense-modalities; it is merely the term "magnetic sensations" that has turned out to be inappropriate; they had formed a wrong hypothesis about the physical cause of their sensations". But nobody even considered saying this; it was decided that the patients had just been indulging in the sort of pointless talk that hysterics often do indulge in. This decision just to drop the idea of magnetic sensations and to ignore the patients' 'reports' of them was taken after a much smaller breakdown of the ordinary connexions than we are asked to tolerate when it is attempted to apply sensation-concepts to automata or to disembodied existence.

Denying sense to the attempt to think of feelings, sensations, emotions, etc., apart from a living organism may seem to be practically the same as denying disembodied mind altogether. Such a denial does not follow, nor has it historically always been held to follow. Aquinas, for example, believed that there were wholly disembodied intelligences, but that they were not liable to any such experiences as seeing and hearing and feeling afraid and having a pain: the evil spirits in hell are tormented not by aches but by the frustration of their wicked will. (Ia q. 54 art. 6, q. 59 art. 4, q. 64 art. 3.) Sensuous experiences are possible only in connexion with a living organism (Ia q. 77 art. 8). Only since Descartes has the main problem become: "How is *cogitatio* related to bodily processes?" ("*cogitatio*" covering, for him, everything 'in the mind', from a toothache to a metaphysical meditation); the old problem was rather: "How can a being that thinks and judges and decides *also* have sensuous experiences?" It was 'intellectual' acts like judgment, not just *anything* that would now be called 'conscious-

ness', which seemed to Aquinas to be wholly incom-
mensurable with events in the physical world; for him,
the 'unbridgeable gulf' was at a different place. The
usefulness of historical knowledge in philosophy, here
as elsewhere, is that the prejudices of our own period
may lose their grip on us if we imaginatively enter into
another period, when people's prejudices were different.

26

THE FALLACY OF
"COGITO ERGO SUM"

IT IS WORTH WHILE to show what is really
wrong with the Cartesian *"cogito ergo sum"*. Many
people find this part of Cartesianism attractive when
they begin studying philosophy; and many unphilo-
sophical people think that such uses of "I" as in "I am
feeling hungry, and remembering what I was thinking
about yesterday" can enable us straightway to understand such a question as "shall I still be conscious
after the destruction of my body?" The idea is that
introspection can give the word "I" a special sense,
which each of us can learn on his own account. "I" in
this sense would not mean the man P.T.G., when
P.T.G. used it; for nobody would wish to know whether
the man P.T.G. was still there after his body was
destroyed. What is supposed is that P.T.G. can use
"I" to express knowledge of something distinct from
the man P.T.G., which is directly discernible to one
who gazes within himself.

Let us begin by reminding ourselves how "I" is used

in ordinary life with psychological verbs. If P.T.G. says "I see a spider" or "I feel sick", people will ordinarily think that the speaker who says this, P.T.G., sees a spider or feels sick. The word "I", spoken by P.T.G., serves to draw people's attention to P.T.G.; and if it is not at once clear who is speaking, there is a genuine question "Who said that?" or "Who is 'I'?" Now consider Descartes brooding over his *poêle* and saying: "I'm getting into an awful muddle—but who then is this 'I' who is getting into a muddle?" When "I'm getting into a muddle" is a soliloquy, "I" certainly does not serve to direct Descartes's attention to Descartes, or to show that it is Descartes, none other, who is getting into a muddle. We are not to argue, though, that since "I" does not refer to the man René Descartes it has some other, more intangible, thing to refer to. Rather, in this context the word "I" is idle, superfluous; it is used only because Descartes is habituated to the use of "I" (or rather, of "*je*" and "*moi*") in expressing his thoughts and feelings to other people. In soliloquy he could quite well have expressed himself without using the first-person pronoun at all; he could have said: "This is really a dreadful muddle!", where "This" would refer back to his previous meditations. (We have here an example of the puzzling *demonstratio ad intellectum* which I mentioned in §15.)

Moreover, what is going to count as an allowable answer to the question "What is this 'I'?" or "Who then am I ?"? These questions might have a good clear sense in certain circumstances—e.g. if Descartes had lost his memory and wanted to know who he was ("Who am I?" "You are René Descartes"), or if he knew that somebody had said "I'm in a muddle" but not that it was himself ("Who is this 'I'—who said he was in a muddle?" "You did"). The states of mind that would give the questions sense are queer and uncommon, but they do occur. But no such rare circumstance was involved in Descartes's actual meditation; in the actual conditions, it is simply that the questions "Who am I?" "Who is this 'I'?" are deprived of any ordinary use and no new use has yet been specified.

When William James tried to pose Descartes's question to himself, and to answer it, he came out with the answer that what he meant by "I", his 'Self of selves', was a collection of feelings in his head and throat. Now of course "I am getting into an awful muddle", said as a soliloquy, did not mean to William James "These head-and-throat feelings are getting into an awful muddle". But how did he manage to make such a mistake? Unlike Descartes, William James was a skilled and trained professional psychologist; how did he manage to miss his own genuine 'Self of selves' when he took an inward look, and only happen upon head-and-throat feelings? If even a professional psychologist can make such a gross mistake, who can be sure of avoiding such mistakes? Who can give directions to make it at least likely that my inward glance will hit upon my real 'Self of selves'? How shall I know when I have glimpsed it? How do I know that you have discerned yours? Am I to take your word for it? And why should I take your word? I may be sure you are not deliberately deceiving me; but may you not, like William James, be honestly mistaken?

What I maintain is that if William James said to himself "I am very puzzled about this problem", his soliloquy would not mean either that the man William James was very puzzled or that certain head-and-throat

I

feelings were very puzzled; "I" would not be serving
to show *who* was puzzled. The use of "I" in such
soliloquies is derivative from, parasitic upon, its use
in talking to others; when there are no others, "I"
is redundant and has no special reference; "I am very
puzzled at this problem" really says no more than
"This problem *is* puzzling" (*demonstratio ad intellectum*
again). Similarly "I have (had) frightful pain" really
says no more than "That pain is (was) frightful"; the
question *whose* pain it is does not arise if the remark is
a soliloquy. (This *demonstratio* will be discussed in the
next Section.)

If you insist that the soliloquistic "I" is not redundant
in this fashion, and likewise does not stand for the
human being who is speaking, then it is up to you to
explain your use of "I"; not only do I not yet understand it, but I have positive grounds for suspecting
that your own apparent understanding of it is a
familiar philosophical illusion. People have had the
oddest ideas about words' having to stand for something; "nothing" has been quite often regarded as
naming an entity, or rather nonentity (*cf.* the fourth
of the *Meditations, ad init.*); and I even once read an
author maintaining that "there" in the idiom "there
is" signifies Reality—"there is a snake in the bath"
would mean "Reality has the characterization snake-
in-bath"! For all I know, a German philosopher has
written something like this about the '*es*' referred to
in "*es gibt*": "*das Es steht vor Allem, auch vor Gott; denn
das Es gibt ja auch Gott, wenn* es *einen Gott gibt*". When
you look for something, other than the human being
who speaks, to be the reference of the soliloquist's "I",
you are surely just falling into this ancient trap.

These are the sort of arguments I should deploy

against somebody who thought the Cartesian "*Cogito ergo sum*" afforded a way for him to grasp some immaterial part of his make-up, signified by "I". I have not said, nor do I think, that the only way of getting at a concept of *soul* or *spirit* is the "*Cogito*"; I just wanted to show that the "*Cogito*" at least is a blind alley.

27

DESCRIBING ONE'S OWN SENSATIONS

REJECTING the "*Cogito*", we must look for some other account of first-person psychological judgments. In the last Section I remarked that such judgments are expressible with a demonstrative instead of a first-person pronoun: "This pain is lessening", "this is terribly puzzling", instead of "I am having less pain", "I am terribly puzzled". The question is how we should account for these sorts of *demonstratio*. I shall consider first-person uses of psychological verbs for feelings and sensations. Part of the ground is covered by Wittgenstein's idea of the *Aeusserung*, utterance, of a mental state. "How that hurts!" or "it hurts *here*" would be *Aeusserungen* of pain, serving not to express judgments in which the pain is described but as learned replacements of primitive (animal) pain-reactions. Similarly, "I am *extremely* angry with you!" is not a description of the degree of my anger but a replacement of primitive angry behaviour. (WITTGENSTEIN, Part I, §§244–5.) All the

I*

same, there is such a thing as deliberate description of one's own feelings; and in particular "I had (or: that was) a nasty stab of toothache five minutes ago" can only be so taken, not as replacing a primitive pain-reaction, for there is no way of writhing and groaning in the past tense. (In WITTGENSTEIN, Part II, we find it expressly recognized that the concept of *Aeusserung* cannot be applied to all first-person psychological statements about feelings; see pp. 187–9.) Where there is deliberate description, there is judgment; and that is my problem.

Let us recollect what we said about statements involving *demonstratio ad sensum*. In agreement here with Aquinas, we said that the judgment expressed in "*The* cat is eating *the* liver" did not differ as regards its own content from one expressible as "a cat eats liver"; the references to a particular cat and a particular bit of liver and a particular time come in because the judgment is made in a particular sensory context, of seeing a cat eat liver. The relation of the judgment to the sensory context was what Aquinas called "*conversio ad phantasmata*"; it cannot be mere simultaneity, but we were no better able than he to specify what the relation must be.

Now when I make this judgment about the cat and the liver, it is not the cat and the liver that are parts of my sensory experience, but *my seeing* the cat and the liver.[1] The concept of *cat eating liver* is exercised,

[1] I must here make a protest against the view that there is something wrong about counting sight (and perhaps hearing) as sensation —that the term "sensation" properly applies only to feelings of eye-strain (say) and not to seeing. It so happens that modern English has no native, Germanic, word covering all the senses alike; "sensation", originally a philosopher's word, is all that we have. But this is a trivial accident of linguistic history; in Latin, Greek and Polish,

then, in a context of sensation; my judgment is a judgment about *the* cat and *the* liver because I see them. If we believed in 'inner-sense', we might say in parallel fashion: "In order that I should say "this pain waxes and wanes regularly", it is not enough that I should think of *pain regularly waxing and waning* and the pain be there; the pain must fall before my mind's eye, my 'inner sense', as the cat and the liver fall before my bodily eye." But this is just mythology. All I need in order to judge about the pain is that my thinking of *pain-waxing-and-waning* should stand in the *conversio-ad-phantasmata* relation (whatever that may be) to the pain itself—not to some sensation of 'inner sense', whereby I am cognizant of the pain. Similarly, suppose I momentarily think I have lost my keys, ferret for them in my pocket, and then report: "How odd! A pang of panic came *after* my fingers had actually touched the keys!" The bits of my sense-experience to which there is now *conversio* are the feeling of the keys and the feeling of panic; there is no 'inner' sensation in which I see or feel the panic and discriminate its panicky quality—there is only the feeling of panic itself.

there is a common native word that applies naturally to exercise of all the senses and is not a borrowing by the layman from the discourse of philosophers. Nowadays in vulgar use "sensation" has acquired overtones (as in "I've got a peculiar sensation") that make it sound wrong as applied to seeing and hearing; but this no more shows that philosophers are wrong to use it in the old way for all the senses than one could refute scholastic talk about essence by saying that 'properly', 'in ordinary language', "essence" means essence of peppermint. (This is meant *only* as a defence of calling sight a kind of sensation; I hold no brief for philosophical talk about sensing and sense-data.)

28

SENSATIONS AND PICTURES

LET US NOW consider the utterance (of a follower of Epicurus, say, looking at the Moon): "This looks like a yellow disc one foot across; *ergo*, this *is* a yellow disc one foot across." If we ask what "this" stands for both times, we are already beginning to get off the track. Although in RUSSELL (3) we are told that "this" is logically a proper name and ordinary 'proper names' are not, in reality "this" is not a name at all. (The whole point of a name is that we can use it to talk about the thing named *in its absence*; contrast Swift's learned men, who each carried a pedlar's pack of the things they needed to talk about.) What gives the word "this" its use is the sensation that the speaker has—his seeing (as it were) a yellow disc a foot across; but "this" is not the name of the sensation, nor is it the name of a 'private' object of which the speaker is cognizant in having the sensation. The speaker has the thought of *a yellow disc a foot across*; the concepts exercised in this thought are primarily applied to physical objects; and what gives his exercise of these concepts a particular application is a certain bit of his sense-experience—of his visual sensations. This last sentence would serve as an account both of his judgment in "This *looks like* a yellow disc a foot across", and of his judgment in "This *is* a yellow disc a foot across". Where, then, does the difference between them lie? Both the thought and the *conversio ad phantasmata* seem to be the same.

Many philosophers have maintained that "yellow

disc a foot across" is understandable primarily as a description of a 'private' object, a 'sense-datum'; "a foot across" must of course then be taken as standing for a 'visual magnitude', not for a relation to the Standard Yard. The judgment expressed in "this looks like a yellow disc a foot across" would be the primary one, at least in theory; it would simply apply to the 'private' object, given in my sensation, concepts of qualities that it possesses. The seemingly simpler judgment expressed in "this *is* a yellow disc a foot across" would really be more complex; it would be to the effect that my 'sense-datum' stood in a relation R to some physical object; my Epicurean would moreover be rashly predicating of the physical object what he had originally predicated of his sense-datum. What relation the relation R might be would be a matter for philosophical enquiry (a matter on which many volumes have in fact been written).

My own view is the reverse of this: that "this looks like a yellow disc a foot across" is not only a more complex expression, but also the expression of a more developed sort of judgment, than "this is a yellow disc a foot across". In the former case, the concepts being exercised, which we acquire in their application to physical things around us, have a transferred or analogical use, serving here to describe the sensation itself. There is no 'sense-datum' language for what I see, and no reason to believe that one could be constructed; we can describe our visual sensations only by describing how it looks as though things were—applying in this description certain of the concepts we use in describing physical things, viz. concepts of shape, size, spatial relations, and colours. I believe that one reason for assuming a distinct realm of sense-data is as follows: "What I actually see is completely describable in terms of shape, size, spatial relations, and colours; physical objects are not completely describable in those terms; *ergo*, what I actually see is never a physical object." (This argument is pretty plainly to be seen in Berkeley's *Three Dialogues*.) But this 'syllogism' is a mere paralogism. The word "describable" might have warned us to look for buried *oratio obliqua*; and the fallacy ceases to be plausible when the *oratio obliqua* is unburied. From the restated premises: "I can completely answer questions as to how the things I see look, in terms of shape, size, space-relations and colours; I cannot completely answer questions as to what physical objects are like, in those terms": it does not even seem to follow that none of the things I see are physical objects, so that they must belong to some other realm. The description of the look of things, in which I use words for shapes, colours, etc., is not a description of queer objects that really have such shapes and colours, but *only* of the look of things, of my sensations. Not that, when I look at the Moon, there is a sensation, a state of my mind, which is round, yellow, and a foot across; but: I am having sensations like seeing a (real) object which is round, yellow, and a foot across. And the *only* way to describe these sensations is to mention physical properties in this sort of way; the analogy is irreducible—there is nothing to the sensation except what it represents something as being.

Our transferred use of language in describing sensations may be compared to our way of describing pictures by what they represent. We might think that "That is a man, and that is his eye", when said of a picture, really meant something like "Somebody drew

this with the intention that *that* should represent a
man and *that* his eye"; in fact, however, a young child
learns the use of pictures and learns the transferred
use of words whereby "man" and "eye" are applied to
bits of pictures, long before it has any power of
formulating such a complex concept as *intention to
represent*. (It is one of the big differences between men
and brutes that brutes take no notice of pictures as
such.) The child, moreover, is not at all likely to get
mixed up between "eye" meaning an eye and "eye"
meaning a drawing of an eye. The use of shape and
colour words to describe sensations is like their use to
describe pictures. The difference is that we can describe
the picture as a physical object, not as a picture,
e.g. by saying it is a set of pencil lines with certain
geometrical attributes; whereas we cannot replace the
mention of colour in describing a sensation, by mention of some inherent quality that represents the
colour (as various black-and-white designs represent
colours in printed books about heraldry). It seems as
though we could say nothing about what visual sensations are like on their own account (*formaliter*, as
Descartes would say); only about the attributes they
represent things as having (attributes that Descartes
would say were in the sensation *obiective*). A sensation is like a picture in no medium; and isn't this
impossible?

But we can after all say something about sensations
formaliter. A sensation, for instance, has a place in the
physical time-scale (in a way that thoughts have not).
It always makes sense to say of a sensation, or of any
bit of sensory experience, like a feeling of fear, that it
lasted continuously all the while that the hands of a
watch moved over a certain space; sensations thus

have their being in physical time—in the time of local motion of bodies. It is not merely that in our sensations there is a representation of physical events as going on in time and occurring one after the other; sensations themselves take up time and occur at different times. If I have sensations of (a flash of red followed by a flash of blue), the sensation of the blue flash really, *formaliter*, follows that of the red flash; and hearing a prolonged note is really, *formaliter*, a prolonged hearing of a note.

Again, just as the pictures of parts of a thing are parts of the picture of the thing, so it might well be held that the seeing of a complex whole is itself *really* complex and composed of parts. Suppose that part of what I am seeing is obscured by an opaque object that comes between, may we not reasonably say that part of my seeing goes on (the seeing of the still unobscured parts) when another part ceases? Or again, consider double vision. Sense-datum philosophers have argued that there must be two sense-data in this case; may we not at any rate say that there is something, my seeing, that splits into two when I push my eyeball, and afterwards fuses together again? It does seem to me to be reasonable to say this sort of thing. (See also MCTAGGART, pp. 96–7.) And if so, sensations would be *formaliter*, really, composed of parts, and really capable (as in double vision) of dividing and then fusing again.

But though time-determinations (and division into parts, if I am right) can really be ascribed to sensation—we are not just saying that it represents physical entities as having such attributes—nevertheless we are not saying the same thing when ascribing them to sensation as when we apply them in the physical world; even here we have an analogous extension of a concept. As I said before, the great thing about such analogous extensions is to know how far the analogy can be carried—to know when to stop. And, although there is much more to say on the problems raised in this work, I am going to stop here.

APPENDIX

HISTORICAL NOTE ON §11:
AQUINAS AND ABSTRACTIONISM

SOME PEOPLE may have been a good deal surprised at my using arguments adapted from Aquinas to refute abstractionism. Aquinas is very often regarded as an abstractionist, and many of his professed followers are abstractionists; and of course he does use the term "*abstractio*" for the process of forming concepts. All the same it can be decisively shown that in his maturest work, the *Summa Theologica*, his views are opposed to what I have called abstractionism.

In accepting the comparison whereby the *intellectus agens*, the mind's concept-forming power, is likened to a light that enables the mind's eye to see the intelligible features of things, as the bodily eye sees colours, Aquinas is careful to add that this comparison goes on all fours only if we suppose that colours are generated by kindling the light—that the light is not just revealing colours that already existed in the dark (Ia q. 79 art. 3 ad 2 um). Furthermore he says that when we frame a judgment expressed in words, our use of concepts is to be compared, not to seeing something, but rather to forming a visual image of something we are not now seeing, or even never have seen (Ia q. 85 art. 2 ad 3 um). So he expresses anti-abstractionist views both on the formation and on the exercise of concepts.

130

Again, an abstractionist, as we say, cannot allow that we possess 'proper' concepts of the various kinds of material substance in our environment, and it is arguable that he ought to reject the term "substance" as nonsensical. But it is a main thesis in Aquinas's theory of knowledge that what our understanding grasps primarily and most readily is the specific nature (*quod quid est*) of material substances, in spite of his also holding that the senses are in no way cognizant of this nature. In fact, he greatly exaggerates the ease and certainty of this knowledge; as when he says that the term "stone" signifies the nature of stone as it is in itself, since it expresses the definition of stone, by which we know what stone is (Ia q. 13 art. 8 ad 2 um). His *soi-disant* followers who adopt abstractionism have been obliged to reject his epistemology on this cardinal point; how they can think that this departure is not fundamental I have never understood.

BIBLIOGRAPHY

AQUINAS, St T., *Summa Theologica*

CHURCH, A., 'On Carnap's Analysis of Statements of Assertion and Belief', *Analysis*, Vol. 10, 1950. Reprinted in *Philosophy and Analysis*, ed. M. Macdonald, Blackwell, 1954

FREUD, S., *Basic Writings*, The Modern Library, New York, 1938

HUMPHREY, G., *Thinking*, Methuen, 1951

JAMES, W., *The Principles of Psychology*, Macmillan, 1901

McTAGGART, J. E., *The Nature of Existence*, Vol. II, Cambridge, 1927

PRICE, H. H., *Thinking and Experience*, Hutchinson, 1953

QUINE, W. V. O., (1) *Methods of Logic*, Routledge and Kegan Paul, 1951
(2) *Mathematical Logic*, Harvard, 1951
(3) *From a Logical Point of View*, Harvard, 1953

REACH, K., 'The Name Relation and the Logical Antinomies', *Journal of Symbolic Logic*, September 1938

RUSSELL, B., (1) *The Problems of Philosophy*, Home University Library
(2) *Philosophical Essays*, Longmans, 1910
(3) 'Knowledge by Acquaintance and Knowledge by Description', Aristotelian Society, *Proceedings*, 1910–11
(4) *An Inquiry into Meaning and Truth*, George Allen and Unwin, 1940

RYLE, G., *The Concept of Mind*, Hutchinson, 1949

WITTGENSTEIN, L., *Philosophical Investigations*, Blackwell, 1953

INDEX